A Short History of Sonoma

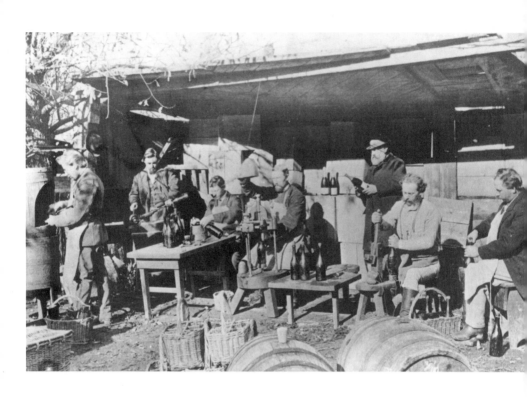

A SHORT HISTORY OF

Sonoma

LYNN DOWNEY

UNIVERSITY OF NEVADA PRESS RENO & LAS VEGAS

University of Nevada Press, Reno, Nevada 89557 USA
Copyright © 2013 by University of Nevada Press
All rights reserved
Manufactured in the United States of America
Design by Kathleen Szawiola

Library of Congress Cataloging-in-Publication Data

Downey, Lynn, 1954–
A short history of Sonoma / Lynn Downey. — 1st ed.
p. cm.
Includes bibliographical references and index.
ISBN 978-0-87417-912-5 (pbk. : alk. paper) — ISBN 978-0-87417-913-2 (ebook)
1. Sonoma County (Calif.)—History.   2. Sonoma County (Calif.)—Biography.
I. Title.
F868.S7D69 2012
979.4'18—dc23   2012034915

FIRST PRINTING
22   21   20   19   18   17   16   15   14   13
5   4   3   2   1

Frontispiece: Bottling at the Buena Vista Winery, 1870s.
Courtesy Sonoma Valley Historical Society. Used by permission.

FOR MY PARENTS

Harvey Orion Downey Jr.
1925 – 2005

Evadne Lee Pickering
1928 – 1985

Contents

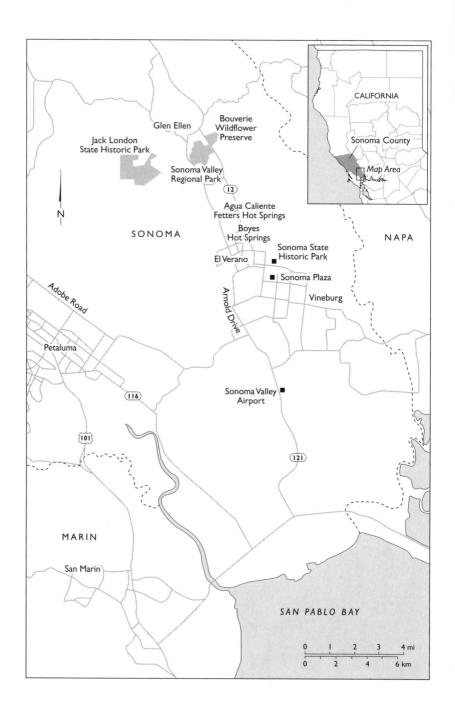

Preface

When I was in junior high school, my grandmother told me a story about the afternoon she had tea with Charmian London, widow of Jack London, the famous author. I remember being amazed at how casually she dropped the London name. I was a budding historian by this time, and her tale added to my already strong interest in Sonoma's history, because it was my own family's history, too.

Both of my paternal grandparents' families arrived in the Sonoma Valley around 1913 from points north and east, and my father was born in his great-grandmother's house just a few blocks from the city's storied central plaza. I grew up in nearby Marin County, and my parents, my sister, and I spent many weekends visiting the folks in Sonoma. As soon as I was old enough, I regularly deserted the family gatherings to wander through the coolness of the adobe mission, marvel at the Victorian furnishings at General Vallejo's home, or—eventually—breathe in the scents of ancient wine casks on the tour of the Sebastiani Winery. The historical pleasures of the Sonoma Valley never paled, and these excursions helped me realize that history was my calling.

Now, a few decades later, I have a career as a historian and writer, and after many wanderings, I also live in Sonoma. I always wanted to write about this place, and finally got the opportunity after a chat with Matt Becker, acquisitions editor at the University of Nevada Press, who was looking for authors to write short histories of western places. I suggested Sonoma, with me as the writer.

In this book, I detail the broad sweep of Sonoma's history, from its earliest native tribes to its Spanish missionary period to its development as a world-renowned wine region. Throughout, I describe its fascinating people and tell the stories that link this city to national and international movements.

The names "Sonoma Valley" and "Valley of the Moon" refer to the town of Sonoma itself and the nearby communities of Glen Ellen, Boyes Springs, Agua Caliente, El Verano, and Fetters Hot Springs. As readers will learn, these places have lived in Sonoma's pockets for more than a century, and locals consider them part of the valley as a whole.

When viewed from the air, the town of Sonoma looks a bit like a cup. Attached to it is Highway 12, threading north with the resort towns along each side, like a very long handle. To me, Sonoma's story works best when you hold the cup and its handle together, so that is what I have done.

Writing this book sent me back into the past I read about as a child and at the same time gave me a chance to learn quite a few new things about my ancestral home. It also put me in touch with a lot of wonderful people whose help and encouragement made it all possible.

Diane Moll Smith, director/curator of the Sonoma Valley Historical Society Depot Museum, opened up the archives and her incredible memory to help me plumb the details of Sonoma's history. Gracious, knowledgeable, funny, and smart, Diane made my work easy and fun as she let me roam free in the society's archives. Her partner in history, office manager Sandi Hansen, was equally generous and helpful.

The other living historical resource in town is Bob Parmelee, whose own book, *Pioneer Sonoma,* served as my early reference material.

Thanks also to Carol Dodge of the California State Parks, and Caitlan Maxwell, of the Montana Historical Society, for their friendly assistance with photo research.

When it comes to Jack and Charmian London, the fount of all knowledge is Sue Hodson, curator of literary manuscripts at the Huntington Library. Sue is always generous with her time and expertise, and she let me tap into her vast reservoir of London lore without complaint.

For his all-encompassing knowledge of California history, especially the Bear Flaggers, I owe much gratitude to my friend and colleague Robert Chandler.

Patti Elkin was the first person to hear every chapter as it came out of the printer. Jeanne Hangauer and Taina Kissinger worked their digital magic for me once again. And Joseph T. Silva graciously allowed me the use of one of the photos in his vast collection of Americana.

Chapter 4 of this book, "A Vine Tradition," is dedicated to the memory of my friend Montse Navines, *mi amiga de la viña*. Montse loved and revered every aspect of winemaking, from vineyard to glass, and I will always remember the food, wine, and fun we had when she visited me in Sonoma from her home in Spain.

And finally, I am grateful to the members of my family who had the good sense to move to Sonoma a century ago: Lewis and Maybelle Bonsey, Albert and Lucy Jane Converse, and Leroy and Mollie Downey.

A Short History of Sonoma

An early-twentieth-century panorama of Sonoma, the Valley of the Moon.
Collection of the author.

Introduction

*T*ourists and other travelers come to the city of Sonoma, California, today for its fine food, award-winning wines, and beautifully land-scaped central plaza. They can also visit the state historic park and its renovated mission, barracks, and old adobe homes, which exist side by side with trendy boutiques and old-fashioned bars. These contrasts make Sonoma—also called the Valley of the Moon—one of the state's most popular vacation destinations.

However, even the most dedicated reader of historical plaques might not realize how important Sonoma has been to the growth and develop-ment of both California and the United States. At the same time, Sonoma was, and still is, a typical American small town, with fraternal organiza-tions, schools, parades, and storefront firms dealing in clothing, jewelry, candles, and locally made French bread. Until about thirty years ago it even had a drugstore with a soda fountain.

Once the last outpost of one of the greatest empires on earth, Sonoma was first wrested from the native inhabitants by Spain, ceded to Mexico, and then claimed by Americans in a revolt that led to California's admis-sion to the Union. Sonoma held a mission centennial celebration in 1923, but the region was first home to a variety of native tribes: Miwok, Pomo, Patwin, and Wappo. In 1823 Sonoma was chosen to be the site of the twenty-first Franciscan mission in the future state of California.

Mission San Francisco Solano turned out to be the last mission ever built in California, and the only one founded under the authority of Mexico, newly independent from Spain.

The actual pueblo of Sonoma began twelve years later when General Mariano Guadalupe Vallejo, the former military commandant at San Francisco, was ordered to Sonoma to set up a presidio to thwart the ambitions of the Russians, settled sixty miles away at Fort Ross. Vallejo was also the administrator of the now privatized mission, and within a few years he would be the military governor of Alta California and the holder of enormous tracts of land throughout the present-day county. He settled his family in Sonoma and never left.

Sonoma in the Mexican era was a heady mix of fine horses and daring riders, theater, dancing, and church bells. Indian labor, disease, and death were also part of the picture. Although native peoples were treated better by the Spanish than by immigrants from other countries, that isn't saying much. Unfortunately, life for the former First Peoples did not improve when the Americans began to take over Sonoma and California.

In the early 1840s government explorer John C. Frémont thought that the United States should have control of California. Under his prodding, a group of very un-military-like men decided to "take" Sonoma for America in June 1846. It was one of the most unusual, and unusually named, American uprisings: the Bear Flag Revolt. The slightly inebriated mob took General Vallejo hostage, fashioned a rudimentary flag designed with a bear that looked suspiciously like a pig, and declared a "California Republic."

The Stars and Stripes followed the Bear Flag up the pole in the central plaza, and soon American soldiers were rubbing shoulders with their Mexican counterparts. They also began to share the delights of the city, which now included fine goods carried by local merchants.

Sonoma wasn't just a military outpost. A few Americans had met Mexico's requirements for residency and set up shops on the central square, trading needed goods for produce and hides. When news of the Gold Rush blew into town, they were ready to supply the locals who temporarily deserted Sonoma Creek for the American River. Sonoma was ready when California became a state in September 1850.

Sonoma had commercial and cultural links beyond its borders, even before statehood. Steamships puffed across the bay from San Francisco to nearby Schellville and Wingo, where horses and later trains brought travelers into town. The Civil War was a concern to citizens, but it didn't slow down life or business, both of which thrived as the century went on. Early writers such as the humorist "Squibob" raved about Sonoma in San Francisco newspapers.

Sonoma's beginnings as a Mexican town meant that it grew up around a central square or, as residents call it (sometimes testily), the Plaza. It's the center of life in town today, but it wasn't always so. One early resident who arrived in town in 1922 said that the Plaza was nothing more than a hayfield with troughs for watering your horses. Hayfield or no, businesses, historic buildings, the mission, and the former military post have surrounded the Plaza for 175 years. Some were lost to time, the elements, or development. But some—like the mission, the home of General Vallejo's brother Salvador, and the former barracks—were rescued from oblivion by historically minded citizens. These sites still fascinate tourists today.

The Sonoma City Hall and the former Carnegie library anchor everything else on and around the Plaza. Firms such as the Schocken and Poppe stores, Ruggles music store, Simmons drug, and other mercantiles were important Plaza residents for many years. There has been a movie theater on the Plaza since the early twentieth century, and the 1933 Sebastiani Theatre serves as the area's art house and the venue for the Sonoma Valley Film Festival.

There's a popular saying in some parts of the wine country: "Sonoma means wine—Napa means auto parts." The viticultural rivalry between these two appellations is palpable today, but no one can dispute the fact that Northern California's wine industry began in the Valley of the Moon.

California's first grapes were planted by Franciscan missionaries, and Mission San Francisco Solano had acres of vineyards located throughout its property. The Vallejo brothers kept vines in many valley locales. But the roots of the wine industry itself began with a "count" (he wasn't really) from Hungary, Agoston Haraszthy. Before buying land and vineyards in Sonoma in 1857 and founding Buena Vista, the state's first commercial winery, he had a variety of adventures on his way across the country. In California alone these included a stint in politics in San Diego and a slightly tarnished career at the San Francisco Mint. Other wineries followed Buena Vista, but it wasn't all smooth sailing for local vintners. The *Phylloxera* parasite ravaged the vineyards in the 1870s, and the miraculous rebirth of Sonoma's wine industry at the end of the nineteenth century, and again in the post-Prohibition era, is a thrilling risen-from-the-ashes story.

The writer Jack London and his equally talented wife, Charmian, were always considered residents of the Valley of the Moon, even though they technically lived outside Sonoma proper, in the village of Glen Ellen, about seven miles from the Plaza. But ask any longtime resident of Sonoma if he or she feels Jack can be claimed as one of Sonoma's own, and you'll get a resounding yes. London's life as a Sonoma rancher is not as well known as his writerly adventures, and fans know even less about Charmian. But both of the Londons contributed much to the life, landscape, and culture of the Sonoma Valley.

The Valley of the Moon includes a few communities whose fortunes are not tied to the town's early years, but their history is very much a Sonoma story. The names are a clue to their fame: Agua Caliente, Boyes Hot Springs, Fetters Hot Springs, El Verano. Located near natural

A 1909 postcard of boaters at Boyes Hot Springs Resort. Collection of the author.

A view of Broadway, Sonoma's main street, in the first decades of the twentieth century. Courtesy Sonoma Valley Historical Society. Used by permission.

springs, these tiny locales were the first places in the valley to be targeted by out-of-towners, even before wine put Sonoma itself on the map.

Fine resort vacations began in these towns, which line up one after the other along Highway 12. For the most part, visitors were the wealthy and overfed residents of San Francisco, who basked in the summer sunshine, away from the city fogs. Taking dips in, and drinks of, the mineral-infused waters made for a pleasant holiday or a temporary cure for rheumatism. Between Sonoma and the springs, visitors could go dancing, see a movie, take a long walk, swim, go boating, or just sit. The area became so well known that a number of songs in the 1920s and 1930s were written about "the Valley of the Moon."

Tourism in Sonoma today is about wine, fine food, relaxation, and history. Luxury hotels, bed-and-breakfasts, and spas are what people come for, but few know that the valley has been offering these amenities to the weary for more than a century. Artists, writers, entrepreneurs, the curious, and seekers of beauty have all found their way to Sonoma.

Sonoma is a deceptively sleepy town; its pace is so relaxed that it is sometimes called "Slow-Noma." History and tradition are treasured here, but the city does not rest on its laurels. Sonoma is a modern American town, firmly planted on the continuum of past and future.

Chapter One

The Village of Huchi

$\mathcal{T}$he front page of the June 30, 1923, issue of the *Sonoma Index-Tribune* featured an eye-catching boldface headline: "Mission Centennial Starts Today." The paper was filled to capacity with articles about the many activities planned for the five-day event, commemorating the establishment of Mission San Francisco Solano by the government of Mexico in 1823. There was a Spanish Ball, a mission play (complete with special lighting effects), brass bands, a rodeo, and music by Capelli's Musical Chicken Pickers. The celebration culminated on "the glorious Fourth," with more brass bands, a speech by Congressman Clarence F. Lea, another rodeo, and a grand ball.

Sonomans were proud of their history, which to them began with the mission's founding a hundred years earlier. And although "Indians" made an appearance in the mission play, no one knew much about the area's original inhabitants, or the centuries of tradition practiced in their valley before the first Europeans arrived.

BEFORE 1769, the year when the first mission was established in San Diego, more than 300,000 Indians lived in what is now California, and they represented as many as a hundred unique cultures. Each of these groups, called tribes or "non-political ethnic nationalities," shared some cultural characteristics, and there were also similarities in language, but they were not unified at all.

These peoples grouped themselves into villages, or "tribelets," made up of families who lived and worked together to find food, observe important rituals, and travel to different locales during specific seasons of the year, sometimes called the "annual round." These family groups could include as few as fifty individuals or as many as five hundred.

Sonoma had been an important border area between a number of Indian groups for centuries: the Patwin, who ranged over three hundred square miles around the present-day city; the Miwok, from the Coast Range, Marin County, and just-adjacent portions of Sonoma County; the Pomo, from the area of the Russian River Valley and the adjacent coastline; and the Wappo, from north of Glen Ellen and up to Clear Lake. Sonoma Creek was the water source for a number of local villages, the most important of which were Huchi and Wugilwa. Although they were similar with respect to living conditions and diet, the different Indian groups who lived near the Sonoma Valley had their own cultural characteristics.

The Patwin, called Tulukal in the nearby Napa Valley, had a rich oral tradition of legends and stories, and believed their spiritual leaders had great healing powers. They had main and "satellite" villages, which were usually located along waterways, and they were sometimes called the "river people." Their boats were made of river reeds called *tule,* and they used the great variety of plant materials on local waterways to make their baskets.

The Miwok lived over a vast area in northern California, from the Sierras to the coast. Those who lived in and near Sonoma were the Coast Miwok, or Tchokoyem. Each geographic group made baskets unique to its locale, and its designs were often similar to those of peoples of nearby groups such as the Patwin and the Pomo. Clothing, ceremonies, and language were also unique to each group. The Miwok who lived near the ocean had sophisticated systems for harvesting fish and other seafood.

Pomo Indians were not a large organized tribe, as many of the other peoples were. Even with shared culture and similar language, the different groups governed themselves in unique ways. In contrast to neighboring tribes, they had a sophisticated trading system with the Russians at Fort Ross after it was established in 1812. Their basketry designs are considered among the most sophisticated in California.

The Wappo called themselves Miyakmah; the Wappo designation came from the Spanish word *guapo,* meaning handsome. The Miyakmah ancestral lands were in the Napa Valley north and west to the Alexander Valley on the Russian River. According to surviving accounts, the Wappo were both good-looking and rather fierce, and they also had a tradition of basket making. Their dances shared similarities with those of the Pomo.

In the area around the Sonoma Valley and outlying regions, the staple food for all tribes was the acorn, though this was not universal across California. Acorns were gathered locally from the valley oak, the coast live oak, and the black oak. The process from raw nut to final edible product was time-consuming but well worth it, because acorns are very nutritious, especially when combined with meat. More than 50 percent of their calories come from carbohydrates, followed by calories from fat and protein.

Acorns were always gathered in the fall, dried in the sun, and then stored in large baskets. To get them ready to eat, the shells were cracked open to reveal the edible kernels. These were ground to a flour-like consistency in a stone mortar and sifted in a basket. Then came the most important step: leaching out the bitter naturally occurring tannins, the only way to stomach foods made with acorns (anthropology students who try acorn products for themselves will attest to this).

There were a few different ways to get the tannins out after the acorns had been crushed or flattened. One method called for putting them in a basin or basket that contained layers of fine and coarse sand. Water was then poured continuously through the mixture, or the basin was placed in a stream where the water moved freely. The acorns could also be buried in mud for days or weeks.

When this process was completed, the crumbly acorn flour was ready to be made into a type of mush or porridge. First it was combined with water and placed in a basket. Hot rocks were added, and these eventually caused the mixture to boil and begin to cook. Once cooled, the finished product could be eaten, and it was described by some nineteenth-century non-natives as rather bland and slightly nutty.

The leached flour could also be made into a type of acorn bread. It was mixed with a little bit of clay (which also helped remove the tannins) and placed in a pit lined with hot stones and leaves. The dough was placed on the leaves, covered with more greenery and more rocks. A pile of soil was placed on top and the layers were allowed to steam overnight. When done, the soft cooked dough was removed, and once exposed to air, it hardened up, making a heavy, rather sweet "loaf" of bread.

In addition to acorns, Sonoma Valley Indians could choose from a great variety of other plants, as well as game, to supplement their diet. Buckeye, pine, juniper, blackberry, and wild grape were abundant and provided nuts and fruits, while Miner's lettuce, cow parsnip, and clover were the leafy greens of the day. Men hunted elk, antelope, duck, geese, deer, and bear. Sonoma Creek abounded in salmon, trout, and turtles.

These people lived for years beyond time in and around the Sonoma Valley, sometimes in conflict with other groups, but for the most part enjoying the abundance of the landscape and the plant and animal life that made California so appealing to early European visitors. Besides the oaks and other trees, which were used for food sources, the Sonoma hills also had madrone, Douglas fir, laurel, and, unfortunately, poison oak, California's answer to poison ivy. The jury is still out on whether local Indians developed an immunity to the plant and its rash-inducing potential (some tribes used it for basketry or cooking) or just learned to avoid it.

What they couldn't avoid, however, were the military and mercantile ambitions of peoples they didn't even know existed.

ON A WARM LATE JUNE DAY IN 1823, a Spanish priest and a small band of soldiers set off from Mission San Rafael, north of the small settlement called Yerba Buena, the future city of San Francisco. They continued to head north, walking through the hills close to where Highway 101 meanders toward the city of Petaluma today. Father José Altimira, a Barcelona-born missionary who had lived in California since 1820, was looking for a place to start a new mission, and since he didn't find any natural springs in the area, he and the troop turned east. Making their way through more hills, they trekked along a narrow valley that marks two other modern thoroughfares, State Route 116 and Stage Gulch Road.

After camping for the night, they kept on exploring, making it as far as present-day Napa. On July 2 they turned west again, because Father Altimira had made up his mind: his new mission would be planted in the beautiful little valley the Indians called Sonoma.

He wrote in his diary about the area's beauty and practicality. The water in the local creek was "crystalline and most pleasing to the taste, flowing through a grove of beautiful and useful trees." These were "lofty and robust, affording an external source of utility, both for firewood and carriage material." This spot had everything he needed, so on July 4, 1823, Altimira set up an altar and said Mass about seven miles south of the present-day city. The Republic of Mexico now had another foothold in the prize that was California.

This republic was actually only two years old, as Mexico had gained its independence from Spain in 1821. But the new government built on the cultural and military work that Spain had begun in 1769, when the famous Father Junípero Serra founded a Franciscan mission in San Diego. The natural resources and strategically perfect harbors of North America's west coast were perfect for expanding and strengthening Spain's reach in the Pacific Rim. The country's rulers also wanted to keep an eye on the equally ambitious aims of Russia, whose fur trappers were spotted moving slowly south from Alaska. In 1812 they had established Fort Ross on the northern Sonoma coast, about eighty miles from Yerba Buena, where a mission and garrison had been in place since 1776.

The Spanish had a system for setting up shop in new territories. It always involved three institutions: the mission, the presidio (military post), and the pueblo (village), usually established in that order. By 1821 there were twenty missions between San Diego and San Rafael. Mexico had happily thrown off its Spanish shackles when it won its independence, but the tried-and-true method of taking a frontier through the mission-presidio-pueblo model was too successful to abandon.

Missions were under the authority of the Franciscan Order, whose administrators worked out of the College of San Fernando in Mexico City. The Spanish mission concept was simple: move into a strategic region and bring the Catholic faith, agriculture, and crafts to the indigenous people. After ten years (give or take), the mission lands were to be turned over to these converts, now citizens of Spain, beginning a process called "secularization."

In 1821 Father Altimira was in charge of Mission San Francisco de Asís (Saint Francis of Assisi) in Yerba Buena, which was sometimes called Mission Dolores. Indians from the sunnier peninsula farther south had been brought to work there, but they were not used to its persistent fog and swamplike conditions. They sickened while living at Dolores, caught diseases from the soldiers and nearby settlers, and were dying at an alarming rate. In 1817 the ambitious and sharp-tongued Father Altimira came up with a solution to this problem. He suggested to Vicente Francisco de Sarría, the Father Presidente, that they close Dolores and San Rafael and create a new and larger mission farther north. Sarría said he would think about it, and the idea languished.

In 1823 the new government in Mexico City had more to worry about than its missions in faraway California. Father Altimira took advantage of this lull and, ignoring Sarría altogether, went straight to California governor Luis Argüello and told him his idea. Not only was Argüello the padre's friend, but he also wanted to expand Mexican settlement north of Yerba Buena. That spring Father Altimira wrote a report advocating the removal of the two missions, and the civil legislature in Monterey gave its approval, bypassing the missionary administration completely. Father Altimira gathered his escort and headed north at the end of June. When he set up the altar on July 4, he told the assembled Indians that the future site would be called New San Francisco. He then went back to Dolores to face the music.

After some angry words and a few weeks of wrangling, the Father Presidente came up with a compromise. He refused to close San Francisco and San Rafael, but did agree to let Father Altimira start a new mission in Sonoma. It would also be called San Francisco, but named for a seventeenth-century Peruvian missionary instead: San Francisco Solano.

Elated that he was authorized to build his northern mission, Father Altimira went back to Sonoma, where he decided to change the location to a place closer to a water source. In October 1823, on the site of the village of Huchi near Sonoma Creek, he began construction of a wooden chapel, assisted by a few hundred Indians sent from Mission Dolores to help him. On April 4, 1824, the chapel was officially dedicated and twenty-six Miwok children were baptized. San Francisco Solano was the first mission established under the Mexican empire, but no one had any idea that it would be the last one ever built in California.

MISSION LIFE HAD STRICT ROUTINES. In the morning everyone attended Mass, had breakfast, and began to work. Women generally labored in the weaving room, where they made blankets and cloth, and men went into the fields, tended the shops, or worked on the buildings. There was a meal at noon, followed by a siesta and more tasks. After an evening service everyone ate dinner and then retired to bed, with single men and women segregated in separate dormitories. Sometimes married couples or families lived in their nearby villages—called *rancherías* by the Spanish—and came to the mission daily to do their work.

Throughout 1824 more buildings were completed at the mission site, including the priest's quarters, housing for the native converts, and adobe brick yards. Crops were planted and pasturage was chosen for cattle and sheep, which had been brought from other missions to help start Solano's own herds. As was customary with other missions, San Francisco Solano had an *estancia* (ranch) and an *asistencia* (sub-mission) in outlying areas.

Boston artist Oriana Day's rendering of the mission compound, 1879. Courtesy Sonoma Valley Historical Society. Used by permission.

One was called Rancho Santa Eulalia, in present-day Solano County, and by 1825 it was home to the bulk of the mission's livestock.

Missionaries who ran successful operations did so by taking a very hands-on approach, assuming responsibility for tasks beyond the religious ones. If the padres of the California missions had had a job description, it would have included the following skills and responsibilities: agriculture (planting, cultivating, harvesting, and preserving crops), animal husbandry (breeding and slaughtering livestock), animal products management (shearing sheep and carding wool, scraping hides, using tallow), medicine (cultivating herbs, tending the sick), accounting (keeping the books of products sold or traded), as well as the expected spiritual duties (conversion, religious instruction, rituals of birth, marriage, and death, saying Mass).

The mission way of life had been perfected over decades in Spanish territories, and it worked fairly well from the standpoint of the government and the College of San Fernando. But the daily reality for the Indians was something else. Many first showed up at the mission out of sheer curiosity, but once they submitted to baptism, they were considered bound to the mission. And when converts decided that life with the padres wasn't for them, they were astounded and angry to find themselves forced to stay. Sometimes Indians were brought against their will from outlying areas to increase the baptism rolls or to work.

One of the most disruptive effects of mission life on the local Indian tribes was the change in diet. Once baptized, Indians were forced to put aside their traditional foods and foodways. They were now expected to grow unfamiliar crops: barley, peas, and beans for the most part. But they didn't completely give up their accustomed diet, and this was a constant source of friction with mission fathers.

Housing was scarce and overcrowded at Sonoma, and many Indians preferred to return to their *rancherías* at night. Others fled to villages far away from Sonoma but were forcibly returned when they didn't appear at work. Rather than reasoning with the Indians, changing their situation, or accommodating their desires in an effort to win their trust, Altimira responded to their resistance with physical punishment and imprisonment, and was even warned by his superiors about his harsh methods.

By the fall of 1826 Indian frustration boiled over into violent action, and a group of men set fire to the buildings and raided food storehouses.

Father Altimira saw no future for himself in Sonoma. He fled, took refuge at San Rafael, and asked to be transferred to Mission Santa Barbara. He was instead sent to Mission San Buenaventura in southern California. This didn't suit him either, and in January 1828 he secretly made his way to Santa Barbara and caught a ship for Spain. His actions scandalized the missionary hierarchy, since he had not asked permission to leave California. He arrived in Spain a few months later and disappeared from history.

His successor was Father Buenaventura Fortuny, who had been the padre at Mission San José for twenty years. Born in Spain in 1774, he studied to be a missionary at the College of San Fernando in Mexico and was sent to Monterey in 1806. He was known to be strict when it came to his own religious life, but more understanding when it came to how his converts conducted themselves. His work at San José bore this out, as it was one of the wealthiest and best-run missions in California. When he got to Sonoma he surveyed the chaos, and with the help of some sympathetic converts, got to work rebuilding the structures, tending to the crops, and reestablishing the rhythm of mission life. By early 1827 a foundation had been laid for a permanent adobe church, as well as a complex of workrooms, tallow vats, storerooms, and quarters for the padre.

Important buildings in the Spanish and Mexican empires were traditionally constructed of adobe, with tile roofs. Adobe is a very old building material that has been used by myriad cultures for thousands of years. Making it was very simple: mud was mixed with straw or sometimes animal manure, poured into forms, and allowed to dry in the sun. Once in place as walls or flooring, the bricks were very sturdy, but they would crumble if they got wet. A reliable roof was therefore always needed—fired tiles were best—and the exterior was usually covered with a waterproof coating, usually made of plaster mixed with sand and limestone. Not all muds were appropriate for making adobe, though, and too much clay in the soil sometimes caused the individual bricks to crack when they were drying. When the California missions were being built, they were constructed with available materials, and whenever possible, adobe. Sonoma's soil did have quite a lot of clay (just ask any local gardener), but it was still useful for making adobe bricks.

It also worked well for making roof tiles. Sometimes animals were used to trample the mixture of mud and straw to make sure the two elements were thoroughly combined. The tiles were shaped over wooden forms and dried, just as adobe bricks were, then placed into a kiln. Some flat tiles were used for flooring, but curved tiles were always required for a building's roof.

Once protected from the elements, an adobe building was surprisingly strong. It was also comfortable, cool in summer and warm in winter. Portions of the original adobe wall of the Sonoma mission can still be seen at the reconstructed site today. There is also a brick in a display case with the dried paw print of an animal that wandered through the site early in its history: a mountain lion.

AS A TRAINED MISSIONARY, Father Fortuny knew that after ten years the secularization process was supposed to get under way, and the decade mark was fast approaching. Ideally, when a mission was secularized, the padres were replaced by regular parish priests, the Indian converts were released from their obligations to the mission, the lands were converted into a pueblo, and each Indian family would receive property and livestock. However, it didn't always happen this way. Some missions remained in business well after the ten-year mark if they were not forced to convert to a regular parish.

But that would soon change. California governor José María Echeandía issued an order of secularization in 1826, allowing married Indians to leave the missions. Then, in 1830, under pressure from the government in Mexico, Echeandía ordered the missions to release all converts and begin the full secularization process.

Even with this upheaval looming, San Francisco Solano continued to thrive under Father Fortuny's leadership. Records kept for 1831 show that there were 705 people at the mission, a number that included the Indians, soldiers, and settlers. Livestock included 2,500 cattle, 725 horses, four mules, 5,000 sheep, and fifty pigs. For a mission in the northernmost outpost of the Mexican empire, this was quite an accomplishment.

In 1832 the adobe church was almost completed, and though Father Fortuny could be proud of his work, he was now fifty-seven years old and he was tired. He had already asked to be replaced by a younger padre as soon as one was available. In the meantime, there was still plenty to do as 1833 began.

That January a new Mexican governor of California, José Figueroa, toured some of the California missions. He did not feel that the Indians were ready for secularization, and he knew that many residents and soldiers expected to be given the mission lands. He didn't agree with this practice; in his view the land should go to the Indians who had worked it for more than a decade. He put his opinion into a report and sent it to the central government in Mexico. In September Father Fortuny was given permission to leave Sonoma, and he set off for Mission San Diego. After working at the missions in San Luis Rey and San Buenaventura, he died at Santa Barbara in 1840.

His replacement, who had arrived in March, was Father José de Jesús María Gutiérrez, the first padre at Sonoma to be born in Mexico rather than in Spain, around 1801. He inherited a thriving and self-sufficient enterprise: nearly 1,000 Indians who lived in or around the mission, huge herds of cattle, horses, sheep, and goats, and healthy crops of wheat, corn, beans, barley, and grapes. But like Father Altimira, Gutiérrez was not successful with the Indians, and for the same reason. He had no previous California mission experience or even administrative experience, and he was the subject of many complaints. Not surprisingly, his tenure didn't last long. In February 1834 he was transferred to Mission Dolores in Yerba Buena, where he spent five years. His next stop was San Antonio de Padua, and sometime after 1844 he went back to Mexico, where he died in 1850.

When Father Gutiérrez showed up at Mission Dolores, the padre in residence there, Father José Lorenzo de la Concepción Quijas, was sent to Sonoma in his place. He was also a native of Latin America, probably Ecuador, and he was affable, educated, and kindly. He continued the building work started by Father Fortuny, adding another women's dormitory and a storehouse to the complex, and putting the finishing touches on the new church. Word got out to traders, merchants, and explorers that they would receive a warm welcome from the padre at Sonoma.

As Father Quijas was getting into his new routine, Governor Figueroa was struggling with an order he had received from the Mexican government in August 1834. It was the final, unequivocal order of secularization. Resigned to the decision, Figueroa appointed the commander of the fairly new garrison in Sonoma to be the *comisionado* or administrator of San Francisco Solano as it went through this process. Not yet thirty, this already seasoned soldier had moved his family to Sonoma the previous year and was one of the most respected commanders in California. His name was Mariano Guadalupe Vallejo.

General Mariano Guadalupe Vallejo. Courtesy Sonoma Valley Historical Society. Used by permission.

THE MEXICAN MILITARY MAN who did more than anyone to help California become part of the United States was born on America's Independence Day, July 4, 1807. His birthplace, Monterey, was the capital of Alta (Upper) California, then under Spanish jurisdiction. His father, Ignacio Vallejo, a foot soldier, had escorted the famous Father Junípero Serra to Yerba Buena when the presidio and mission were established there in 1776.

Vallejo was lucky enough to be noticed and educated by the governor, Pablo Vicente de Solá. His classmates included two future governors of Mexican California: his nephew Juan Bautista Alvarado and José Castro. The young Mariano learned English as well as other languages when he was tutored by an English merchant living in Monterey, William Hartnell. When Solá was replaced by Luis Argüello in 1822, after Mexican independence, Vallejo became his personal secretary.

A strong military was always needed in California, and a career as a soldier was an attractive option for the men of Monterey. In 1824 Governor Argüello convinced the lively young Vallejo to become a cadet in the local company, and he soon rose in the ranks to corporal. Two years later, at age nineteen, he joined the territorial legislature, which met in his hometown, and he was promoted again, to second lieutenant.

Vallejo's military career was launched in 1829 when he led troops in the first of a number of northern California Indian wars. A Yokut Indian from the San Joaquin Valley named Estanislao—for whom Stanislaus

County was later named—had been raised at Mission San José, but after being given leave to visit relatives in the interior, he refused to return to the mission. He led a group of insurgents in skirmishes against the Mexicans and fought against Vallejo's troops in a three-day battle, which Vallejo eventually won. It was the first of many military campaigns for the young man, in which he learned not only to fight the Indians but also to respect them. In his later years he would try to resolve conflicts through treaties rather than through battles.

In 1832 Vallejo married Francisca Benicia Carrillo, and the following year he was appointed commander of the presidio in Yerba Buena. Vallejo moved his young family to the sandy, flea-ridden fort overlooking the strategically important bay and took up his post with enthusiasm.

In April 1833 Governor Figueroa ordered Vallejo to take an escort of soldiers to Fort Ross, on California's coast. The Russians were encroaching a little too far to the south for Mexico's comfort, and Vallejo was supposed to look for a suitable site for a northern presidio, where the government could keep an eye on them. A few months later, Figueroa told Vallejo that the new military post would be conveniently located where there was already an established mission: Sonoma. Vallejo was then given orders to relocate to Sonoma and establish the presidio himself. The governor sweetened the deal by giving Vallejo additional property in present-day Petaluma, which grew to more than 60,000 acres.

In October 1834 Figueroa also named Vallejo the administrator in charge of secularizing Mission San Francisco Solano. His job was to take the prosperous mission and all of its contents, and divide it into two parts: one for the Indians and the other for the benefit of the future pueblo of Sonoma.

The mission's rich inventory of structures and contents was astonishing. It included all of the vessels for church services, multi-room padre's quarters, a music room, a tool shed and carpenter's shop, a forge, a tannery, numerous granaries, weaving and sewing rooms, a library, an orchard with more than 3,000 trees, a vineyard, 6,000 cattle and the same number of sheep, and 2,000 horses. In addition, there were twenty-seven Indian homes nearby.

When the secularization process was finally completed, the Indians either returned to their *rancherías* or began to work the small plots of land that Vallejo authorized for them. Some stayed in town and worked for Vallejo's brother Salvador, who now also lived in Sonoma. Some of the women became servants in local homes. Over time many of these original inhabitants—Patwin, Miwok, Wappo, and Pomo—were absorbed into Sonoma's population. Until a few decades ago, they were a footnote in Sonoma's history, except in colorful or romanticized tales about the city's past.

In August 1896, for example, the *San Francisco Call* newspaper published an article about a local Indian man named "Vinciente," who was supposedly 115 years old. Born in a village outside of Sonoma, he said he went with others as a child to Monterey to see Father Junipero Serra at his mission near Carmel. The group was apparently not very impressed with what they saw, as they quickly returned to Sonoma. Later, Vinciente was hired by Vallejo to be his servant, and he was quoted as saying, "General Vallejo was the greatest man that ever lived." According to the article, Vinciente now lived fifteen miles from Sonoma and occasionally walked to town.

This account sounds suspicious, but he did exist, though the real details are a bit more believable. Vicente (who later took the last name Carrillo) was born in Sonoma around 1788, which means he couldn't have seen Father Serra, as the missionary died in 1784. An article about his grandchildren appeared in the *Sonoma Index-Tribune* in 1891, and Vicente himself died at age 114 in 1902.

VALLEJO APPOINTED a local man named Guadalupe Antonio Ortega to take charge of distributing the actual mission property, and named his brother Salvador as Ortega's assistant. A notorious hothead, the younger Vallejo clashed with Father Quijas, who had remained in residence, living in the padre's house and conducting services. Salvador dismantled many of the mission buildings to reclaim their bricks, which were then used to build houses or public buildings. According to legend, he once rode his horse through the priest's living quarters. Ortega's debaucheries around town also outraged the priest.

The transition from mission settlement to official pueblo took place in 1835. Vallejo used the name "Sonoma" for the first time in a letter to Governor Figueroa in April, telling him that the work of secularizing the mission had been completed. However, Father Altimira was the first European to commit the name to paper. In his diary of the 1823 exploration, he referred to the valley he visited as "the place called *Sonoma* by the Indians who in other times dwelt there."

His explanation for the original meaning of *Sonoma* was soon forgotten. A generation after the mission was founded, an article in the April 8, 1848, issue of the *California Star* newspaper reported that Sonoma was "named from an Indian chief of some one of the Tulare tribes, and of considerable notoriety."

In the early twentieth century city boosters located other, more romanticized meanings of the word in the memoirs of early residents. One supposedly came from General Vallejo's son Platón, who said that *sono* meant "nose" in the Suisun language, and that Sonoma was named for an early chief who was born with a nose that was rather larger than normal. Another was "Sonomaite," a local, naturally occurring mineral that was actually named for the county long after the town was established.

However, anthropologists have the most likely explanation. In the Wappo language, the suffix *noma* means "place, home or village," and is found in the names of other local villages, such as Anakota-noma, near Mount St. Helena in Napa County. The prefix *tso* means "earth or ground." Put them together and you get *Tso-noma*: Sonoma.

The Sonoma barracks as they appeared in the early 1920s. Collection of the author.

Sonoma Barracks.
Erected in 1836 by Gen. Vallejo at
Sonoma, Calif.

That April, Vallejo was appointed director of colonization for the northern frontier, as well as Upper California's military commandant. And on June 24, 1835, the governor signed the order officially establishing Sonoma as a "presidial" town, the headquarters for the military in the north. Vallejo was ordered to lay out streets, create a central plaza, and begin dividing the area into square lots for future homes and businesses.

First on the agenda, however, was the construction of a fort, "to protect the inhabitants from incursions of savages and all others." This meant the Russians, and likely the Americans as well. In Spanish, a military fort was called a *presidio*. The word comes from the Latin *praesidium* or "pre-settlement," and refers to a collection of soldiers in charge of holding a frontier, a system dating back to Roman times. A two-story soldiers' barracks was hurriedly erected west of the mission, with roof tiles coming from its former kilns and the rubble of its dismantled former workrooms. It wasn't a very imposing structure, but it was serviceable.

By June, Father Quijas had had enough of Salvador Vallejo's insolence and Ortega's bawdy behavior. He left Sonoma for San Rafael, and though he said he would continue to conduct services, he would not live at the mission as long as Ortega was in charge. He was true to his word; he never lived in Sonoma again. As late as 1843 he was overseeing Mission Dolores as well as San Rafael, but he moved to San José when he was promoted to a high administrative post. He went to Mexico in 1844 to talk with his superiors and remained there for the rest of his life.

In 1836 Vallejo was named *comandante general* of California. For the rest of his life he was known as—and styled himself as—"General Vallejo," though his actual rank never ran that high. And in that same year he allied himself with a man from the Suisun tribe who came to be called Chief Solano, and whose strong personality and military prowess matched his own.

The Suisun Indians were a sub-tribe of the Patwin, and by the beginning of the nineteenth century they lived north and east of San Pablo Bay. This area, which rings present-day Marin County, had become a place of refuge for Indians who were fleeing life at the missions. But the Spanish were also spreading out, and clashes were common.

In 1810 Gabriel Moraga, son of José Moraga, who had founded the presidio in Yerba Buena, led a force against a large band of Suisuns.

When the battle was over, Moraga brought a number of children with him to Mission Dolores to be baptized. One of them was an eleven-year-old boy called Sem-Yeto, who was given the name Francisco Solano. In 1824 he accompanied a group of Suisuns being relocated to the mission in Sonoma. He eventually became the civil leader among the Indians at the mission, likely because of his demonstrated leadership skills, and perhaps also because he was nearly six feet seven inches tall. By 1836 he and Vallejo were allied in battle against warring tribes in the Sacramento Valley.

Vallejo formed a personal alliance with Solano, showing a respect for him that was rare in relations between Mexicans and Indians. He gave him a uniform and a horse as a tribute to his importance in keeping order in Sonoma and beyond. Vallejo also took Solano and some of his men with him to a meeting in Monterey to impress his superiors with the kind of power he was wielding. The men fought in more military campaigns together in Napa and Mendocino in 1843.

Solano proved his loyalty to the Vallejo family more than once. An English doctor named Edward Turner Bale lived in Sonoma, and was married to one of the Vallejo nieces, Maria Soberanes. At one time he was the surgeon-in-chief to the provincial army, but he resigned in 1844 (his doctoring wasn't always up to par) and then began spreading rumors about Salvador Vallejo's loose character. In the spring of 1844 the two men got into a fight, which Salvador won, though accounts vary as to whether he used the flat of his sword or a bullwhip to humiliate the medical man. Bale left town and in July he rounded up about fourteen Americans to help him teach Vallejo a lesson.

The men rode into town as Salvador was crossing the Plaza with a friend named Cayetano Juárez. Dr. Bale walked up to Vallejo and took two shots at him with a pistol at point-blank range. One bullet grazed Vallejo's chest and the wadding from the second shot struck Juárez's jaw. As bystanders rushed to the scene, Bale and some of his followers took off to the home of Jacob Leese, Vallejo's brother-in-law, who was also Sonoma's alcalde, a combination of mayor and justice of the peace. When Solano heard what had happened, he gathered a large force of his own fighting men and stormed Leese's house, dragging Bale toward the Plaza and a convenient tree, preparing to lynch him. The general, however, prevented the hanging, and Bale and his supporters were placed in irons.

The charges against Bale were dropped, because the governor did not want to antagonize the English by throwing one of their countrymen in jail, even though Bale had become a Mexican citizen in order to hold property and marry. Bale was banished from Sonoma, and the general asked Salvador to escort his would-be assassin out of town. When Salvador told Bale he would someday repay him for the attempt on his life, the doctor reportedly fell to his knees and asked for forgiveness, which Salvador granted.

In the early 1840s Vallejo arranged for Solano to get a land grant near the mission's former *asistencia* of Santa Eulalia. The petition called Solano "Chief of the Suisuns," and Vallejo always referred to him by this title, which is how his name appears in countless books and articles today. Solano was reportedly married a few times and had many children, but this is hard to verify. He passed out of Vallejo's life and disappeared from the historical record during the Gold Rush. Some scholars feel this is because Vallejo's tolerant attitude toward Indians was not shared by the Americans who overran the area. In 1850, when he was a member of the state legislature, Vallejo persuaded lawmakers to name a county after Solano. The man himself probably died around 1851 and is rumored to be buried near Rockville, close to the site of a former encampment called Yulyul.

Life in Sonoma was not just about soldiery, however. Men like Vallejo, and even the soldiers themselves, enjoyed an ease that had a lot to do with the gentle climate, good growing conditions, and the stable underpinnings of family and the Catholic Church. If an occasional fight broke out, or if a bear was brought into town to fight a bull for entertainment, the citizens couldn't really be faulted. Vallejo ran a tight ship as commandant, but he exemplified the generosity and hospitality that was recorded in the diaries of many foreign visitors. He also cultivated his intellectual side. In 1837 he brought a printing press from Monterey to his Sonoma headquarters, and the following year he used it to reprint an old Spanish medical book.

Vallejo's home on the main Plaza, called Casa Grande, was the social center of town and a place of pilgrimage for the politically and culturally important people of California. According to some accounts, Vallejo was rather stiff in his official capacity as military commander, but warmer in person. He also had a very impressive wine cellar.

When Richard Henry Dana published an updated edition of his book *Two Years Before the Mast* in 1869, he wrote about meeting the young Vallejo when he was in charge of the presidio in Yerba Buena. With the hindsight of history, he wrote that the commandant was very popular with the foreigners who visited California.

This popularity would serve Vallejo well, for in the 1840s a wild card would be dealt to peaceful, yet strategically important Sonoma, changing the city forever.

The Americans were coming.

Chapter Two

The American Era

*C*alifornia history is full of people showing up when they are not wanted. Sonoma's history is no exception, though some were more welcome than others.

Under both Spanish and Mexican law, foreigners who wanted to settle in California and buy land had to convert to Catholicism, give up their former citizenship, swear allegiance to Mexico, and learn Spanish, which most visitors did. Many men also became naturalized citizens and married local women. One of them was Jacob Leese.

This Ohio native was born in 1809, went west to trade along the Santa Fe Trail, and ended up in Yerba Buena in 1836. The little settlement was a good place to make money, since Mexico allowed foreigners to engage in the hide and tallow trade. Locally skinned hides and their by-products were traded for manufactured goods that came off American ships and were then sent into the interior to places like Sonoma.

By July 1836 Leese had finished building his home in Yerba Buena, which also served as his place of business, and which he claimed was the first house built in the fledgling city. He decided to hold a housewarming (and sly Independence Day celebration) on July 4 and invited prominent Mexican citizens from around the area. One was General Vallejo, who came to the party with his sister Rosalía. She and Leese were quickly attracted to each other and after he was naturalized in 1837, he and

Rosalía were secretly married. They worried about the general's reaction to having a Yankee brother-in-law, but after an initial period of disapproval, he came to respect his new relation. Leese and Rosalía moved to Sonoma in 1841 and Vallejo gave them a grant of land called Rancho Huichica, located in the Carneros wine-growing region of present-day Napa County. They also started building a house on the Plaza.

As the 1830s progressed, settlers continued to trickle into California. Some were merchants like Leese, who eventually became large landowners and ranchers. Others were less ambitious: fur trappers, wild mountain men, deserters from American and British ships among them. Another was the Swiss entrepreneur John Sutter.

Born in 1803, Sutter fled a failed life in Europe and made his way to New York in 1834. Heading west to try his hand at trading, he made it all the way to Honolulu before turning back and fetching up in Yerba Buena in 1839. He saw the way the wind was blowing and became a Mexican citizen, which allowed him to obtain a huge land grant at the junction of the Sacramento and American rivers, now part of the city of Sacramento. He called his rancho New Helvetia (New Switzerland) and not only planted crops but built the massive adobe structure that came to be known as Sutter's Fort. It was the center of his farm and trading empire, and was the first stop for travelers and settlers after they crossed the Sierras. Sutter's power rivaled Vallejo's and the two men were never at ease with each other.

The home of Jacob Leese, later the Leese-Fitch adobe, on the Sonoma Plaza. Courtesy Sonoma Valley Historical Society. Used by permission.

Then, in May 1841, everything about life in California began to unravel.

The Mexican government was getting nervous about the rising tide of foreigners—mostly Americans—who were settling in California. The minister of war issued an order that month mandating that all visitors to the area had to come with passports and consular permission. Those who had been in California for years were not immune from this order; they could be expelled if they didn't obtain the retroactive paperwork. This didn't deter very many people, and it also had no effect on the men who showed up simply to take a look around.

In August 1841, for example, the sloop-of-war *Vincennes,* under the command of Cadwalader Ringgold, entered San Francisco Bay. His ship was part of the six-vessel United States Exploring Expedition, a surveying project of the US Navy under the command of Charles Wilkes, who was in Oregon with his own ship. One of the expedition's tasks was to chart the entire west coast, paying particular attention to San Francisco Bay. Throughout the fall the officers of the *Vincennes* left their vessel and headed to a number of inland cities, including Sonoma. And though he did not go there himself, Charles Wilkes wrote up the information he was given by Ringgold and others after their excursion to the valley. His comments appeared in *Narrative of the United States Exploring Expedition,* which he published in 1845.

He referred to the pueblo as "Zonoma," and said it was a large city "upon paper," but that in reality it featured only a few uninspiring buildings. These included General Vallejo's house, Casa Grande, Salvador Vallejo's home, and the "old dilapidated mission-house of San Francisco Solano." He wasn't impressed with Vallejo, but was grateful that the general had offered to supply his men with the wheat, lima beans, potatoes, and other vegetables that they needed. He was even happier when he was able to obtain the supplies elsewhere. He had no desire to be indebted to the general, who he felt was too imperious and considered "every bushel of grain as much at his command as he does the persons of the people, and the property of the state." He acknowledged Vallejo's power in the region, though, and then made a prediction about its future: "The situation of Upper California will cause its separation from Mexico before many years."

In May 1841, the same month that the Mexican government issued the passport order, a large group of settlers under the leadership of Missourian John Bidwell left Kansas for Oregon. At Salt Lake a splinter group led by Bidwell and John Bartleson decided to go to California instead. In November, after a harrowing cross-country trip, they straggled onto the rancho near Mount Diablo belonging to Dr. John Marsh, an American. When they discovered that they needed passports, a group left again for Mission San José, the closest location where they could get any official papers. While on the road they were overtaken by a cavalry troop, which escorted them to the mission. There they faced the man who would decide their fate: General Vallejo.

As military commander he had the responsibility of ensuring order in California, and that included managing the immigrant influx. Already disposed to like Americans, Vallejo agreed to issue the passports to the group. His faith in them was well placed, especially with Bidwell, who would later work with the general in the new state legislature.

The year 1841 also saw the Russians pull out of California. This pleased Vallejo, though he was less enthusiastic when John Sutter purchased Fort Ross (which he had wanted for himself). Vallejo was not shy about expressing his opinion that California would do well under American jurisdiction, and by the end of 1842 he had more opportunity to help this process along.

Captain Thomas ap Catesby Jones was the commander of the US Pacific Squadron, which patrolled the western ports in the 1840s. While at Callao, Peru, in the fall of 1842, he read newspaper reports stating that a conditional state of war existed between Mexico and the United States, thanks to agitation in the independent republic of Texas. There was also a rumor that California had been sold to England for $7 million. With no way to verify the information, Jones left the squadron in Peru and headed to California on his flagship, the *United States,* with the ship *Cyane* alongside.

On October 19, 1842, he entered Monterey harbor. There he met governor Juan Bautista Alvarado, who, unaware that the rumor of war was just that, signed articles of surrender. On October 20 the American flag was raised at Monterey. A stunned Thomas O. Larkin, the US consul, hastened to tell Jones that he was in error, showing him Mexican newspapers that were more recent than the ones he had seen in Peru. On

October 21, an abashed Jones took down the American flag, gathered up the sailors who were wandering around Monterey, and after giving the Mexican flag a salute with his guns, left the bay.

Just before Christmas Jones and an escort came to Sonoma to meet General Vallejo, but that visit was also a comedy of errors. Vallejo sent a party to welcome them, but Jones and his men had headed toward town via the wrong estuary. They ended up at Rancho Huichica, where they were summarily arrested by some local cavalrymen. While in the area Jones saw Chief Solano practicing military maneuvers with his tribesmen for the campaign he and Vallejo would undertake against hostile Indian tribes the following year.

Salvador Vallejo was dispatched to meet Jones and bring him to Sonoma, after which he locked Jones and his escort in the barracks, thinking the worst. The general knew they weren't a threat and got them out around midnight, then welcomed Jones with a fiesta that lasted three days. Vallejo served him the best in local foods, as well as wines and brandy from his own cellars. For entertainment there was a footrace, which was won by a local Indian man, whom Jones rewarded with a gold coin. A few days after he returned to his ships, Vallejo visited Jones on the *Cyane*. The general found no fault with the American, despite his diplomatic bungling, and his conviction that the United States needed to play a role in California's future continued to grow.

In 1842 the civil and military leaders of California were saddled with a new governor, Manuel Micheltorena, appointed out of Mexico City. By the fall of 1844 ousted former governor Juan Bautista Alvarado had enough support to plan his overthrow. Looking to Vallejo for backing, he was shocked when the general dismissed his troops in November, saying that he could no longer afford to maintain them. This allowed Vallejo to stay neutral in what became an ugly internecine war, which ended with Micheltorena's defeat in February 1845 at the Battle of Cahuenga Pass and his replacement by Pío Pico.

This kind of conflict spurred Vallejo and his sympathetic friends to continue speaking about their identity as Californios—that is, people of Spanish descent born and raised in pre-conquest California. The term usually referred to the elite families who controlled large tracts of land under Spanish, and then Mexican, rule. But it also referred to those who took their identity from their residence in California, and not from the country of their ancestors.

Men like Vallejo wanted to be residents of an independent California, free from the dysfunctional politics of Mexico City that were causing upheaval in the region. Upper and Lower California had distinct politics and leaders, they quarreled frequently, and the governors did not always have California's welfare uppermost in their minds. The recent gubernatorial skirmishes between Alvarado and Micheltorena just fueled their desires. They would soon find out that other men—American men—had a similar idea.

JOHN CHARLES FRÉMONT was always restless. The son of a French tutor and a woman who was not his wife (but in fact was the wife of someone else), the sting of illegitimacy never left him. Throughout his life he tried to overcome the humiliation of his beginnings, and swung from spectacular success to abject failure. His secret marriage in 1841 to Jessie Benton, the daughter of powerful senator Thomas Hart Benton, helped catapult him into the prominence he desired. It also made him one of the catalysts for the eventual American takeover of California.

He was an officer in the Corps of Topographical Engineers of the US Army, and in 1843 he led an expedition into California to update the information that Wilkes had gathered two years earlier. He ended up at Sutter's Fort in February 1844 and observed the tenuous hold that Mexico had on the province. He went back to the States and published a report of his adventures. It was well received and piqued the interest of powerful people, including his father-in-law, who proposed that Frémont return to California. By the winter of 1845 he was again at Sutter's Fort.

A few months earlier, the government of Mexico had taken its rules about foreigners even further, and forbade any more immigration from Missouri and Oregon. By this time there were 1,300 people from the United States, England, and other countries within California's borders. Many of them were in the vicinity of Sonoma, as trappers, ranchers, or farmers. In November, military commander José Castro, former governor Alvarado, and their escort came to Sonoma to find out what these foreigners' intentions were. A group of men showed up to hear what the Mexican representatives had to say. They agreed to obey the laws, which included getting the proper paperwork, which many of them did not have. However, some members of the American contingent heard things differently.

One of those was a man named Pat McChristian, who reported on the get-together to settlers who hadn't attended. He said the authorities were going to expel them at the spring thaw and set them loose without livestock or arms. Outraged, and already seething at having to live under the Mexican yoke, they began to talk about occupying Sonoma, the military capital of the north, in order to force America to take California.

In the meantime, events were already snowballing toward the inevitable conflict. In December of 1845 Texas was annexed by the United States, after being an independent republic since 1836. The following month, Frémont was in Monterey, asking Consul Thomas Larkin if he could winter in the San Joaquin Valley. Larkin gave him permission but warned him not to do anything to provoke the Mexicans.

Frémont didn't take Larkin's advice, and in March he was ordered to leave California. He refused, saying that he didn't feel he had to obey an order that was insulting to him as an officer and an American. He then rode toward the Gabilan mountain range of the central coast, where he stopped and raised an American flag on Gavilan Peak (which was later renamed for him). He then received a letter from Larkin, who said that troops were amassing to throw him out. He had no official instructions from President James Polk, but he knew he was not supposed to be irritating the Mexican government. He headed toward Sutter's Fort, but realizing that his antics made him unwelcome, he decided to change direction and march to Oregon, where he stopped at Klamath Lake.

In April, Lieutenant Archibald Gillespie arrived in Monterey, carrying orders from the new president, James Buchanan, for both Larkin and Frémont. Although the men were ordered to be cautious and not to antagonize the local officials, Larkin was aware that sentiments in favor of Americans were growing in Upper California. Even with these worries, former Mexican governor Alvarado held a ball at his Monterey home, which Vallejo and Gillespie also attended. Vallejo suspected that Gillespie was there to keep an eye on the Mexican officers, and actually tried to keep him under surveillance, but Gillespie slipped out of town and went north to see Frémont in Oregon.

Gillespie reported that he had seen what looked like war preparations, and assumed they were a response to American agitation. In reality, what he saw was the coming conflict between Governor Pío Pico and military commander José Castro over the disputed location of the province's capital and the funding of the political and military branches of the government. But Frémont believed Gillespie's interpretation and decided to abandon his Oregon expedition to head back to California and assess the situation for himself.

The following month he was in Bear Valley, where he met up with Ezekiel Merritt, who had been named leader of the band of discontented settlers that congregated around Sutter's Fort. A rough-edged trapper, hunter, and drinker, Merritt was an unlikely leader, but he knew his way around northern California and was adept at stirring up anti-Mexican sentiments in his fellows.

At the beginning of June 1846 Frémont was at Sutter Buttes, a volcanic mountain range about forty miles from Sacramento. Men soon began to gather around to talk about taking California for the United States. Frémont said nothing about supporting them, and spoke as though he wanted to discourage their efforts, which confused them. They had all thought Frémont was on their side, which he actually was; he just wasn't ready to commit to a takeover. At least not one done in his name.

On June 5, General Castro visited General Vallejo in Sonoma. He knew that the possibility of an American takeover of Sonoma was very real. He offered to keep a boat ready in case Vallejo wanted to leave town, but he declined. Instead, Vallejo offered horses and supplies to help Castro in his campaign against Governor Pico. The horses were on the Soscol Rancho in the Carquinez Strait, which straddles today's Solano and Contra Costa counties. Castro dispatched six men to round them up.

Frémont knew about Castro's movements around the north, and told the massed men that the Mexican troops were on their way to the Sacramento Valley to stop the Americans. His intelligence was faulty; Castro was nowhere near Sacramento and the number of men with him was far fewer than the number that Frémont claimed. But the damage was done.

Francisco Arce and José María Alviso were in charge of the troop sent to pick up the horses at Soscol. They decided to take the animals northward through the Sacramento Valley before turning south toward San José, where Castro would be waiting. They crossed the Sacramento River at Knight's Landing, near Grafton in present-day Yolo County. The ferryman, William Knight, knew some Spanish and thought he overheard the men making disparaging remarks about Americans. Knight interpreted these comments to mean that the Mexicans were gathering horses for troops being organized to fight them. He sped to Sutter Buttes, where he knew that Frémont and his discontented compatriots were located.

The news from Knight's Landing was the catalyst that Frémont had been waiting for. He was outraged and was determined to keep Castro from taking delivery of the horses. He therefore dispatched Merritt and a man named Robert Semple, along with a few others, to intercept the Mexicans. Semple, a six-foot, six-inch Kentucky-born dentist and printer, had fetched up in California in 1845 and found himself quickly allied with the sentiments of the Americans.

Arce and Alviso spent the night of June 8 at Sutter's Fort and then headed south. At dawn on June 10 they were confronted by Merritt and his party, who overwhelmed the men and took possession of the livestock. The humiliated Arce and Alviso were allowed to keep their swords, and each member of the troop was given a horse to ride back to San José and give Castro the bad news.

Merritt returned to Frémont's camp on June 11. He now had a plan: gather more men to "commit depradations" and obtain enough horses to supply all American immigrants, so they could go back to the United States. In addition, they would imprison civil and military leaders to force Mexico into starting a war. Once that was under way, Frémont would take California for the United States after uniting the Americans into a fighting force. Twenty men volunteered to undertake the first and most important part of the operation.

Seize Sonoma.

And arrest General Vallejo.

BY NOON ON JUNE 11 the raiding party was back at the Buttes with the horses, and the next phase of the operation soon went into effect. Goaded again by Frémont and his grand plans, an even larger group began to form. Twenty men volunteered to join Merritt and Semple on their mission, among them Granville P. Swift, an early emigrant from the United States to California who was said to be one of the best shots in the West; his friend Franklin Sears; three men named Kelsey and John Grigsby, who were also early California arrivals; William Fallon, a former Frémont employee; an Army deserter named Henry L. Ford; the ferryman William Knight; and William B. Ide, the Massachusetts-born co-leader of an overland party who had arrived only the previous October. By afternoon they were ready to ride.

On their way through the mountain ranges, the men stopped to rest and pick up more raiders. One was William Todd, the cousin of future first lady Mary Todd Lincoln. The others were malcontents stirred up by messengers sent throughout the valleys as the group made its progress, stopping only to rest themselves and their mounts.

Everyone expected Sonoma to be armed to the teeth. Vallejo surely would have filled the presidio with soldiers again, given the increase in military agitation throughout California. The riders moved swiftly and with secrecy, thinking that a formidable force awaited them. By dawn on June 14, when they rode out of the Napa Valley and approached the Sonoma pueblo, the party was thirty-three strong.

Ahead of them was the huge Plaza, which, even at this early hour, should have seen soldiers on patrol or practicing maneuvers. But except for one civilian whom they had taken prisoner as they rode toward town, the area was deserted. Was it possible that the garrison was actually empty? Mystified, the rebels rode toward Vallejo's enormous Casa Grande, dismounted, gathered on the doorstep, and pounded on the door.

The startled general and his wife looked out from their upstairs window and saw what Señora Vallejo later referred to as "bandits" huddled below, wearing buckskins, their heads covered with fur caps or bandannas. The Vallejos also saw how many guns the men were carrying. Ignoring his wife's entreaties to escape out the back, Vallejo put on his old uniform and instructed his servants to open the door to the visitors.

A few of the raiders stumbled into the *sala,* while the rest remained outside. Merritt was identified as the spokesman for the group, and with the dignity and sense of entitlement that had marked his entire life, General Vallejo turned to him and said, "To what happy circumstances shall I attribute the visit of so many exalted personages?" No doubt taken aback by this reception, Merritt told Vallejo that he was under arrest and California was, from that moment, independent.

Vallejo had always thought California should be an American protectorate. However, he was dismayed that it was happening through a takeover, rather than through diplomacy or treaty. He knew there was a real possibility that the situation could turn bloody, and it was up to him to keep that from happening. He told Merritt that the appropriate papers should be drawn up and suggested that his brother-in-law, Jacob Leese, was the man to do the job. Within a few minutes, Leese was brought, under guard, to Vallejo's home. He and Robert Semple prepared what were essentially articles of surrender, which included stipulations guaranteeing the safety of anyone in town who did not try to thwart the takeover.

Always a generous host, Vallejo arranged for wine to be served inside Casa Grande. After some time had passed, John Grigsby came in to check on the negotiations on behalf of the anxious rebels outside. He saw that the captives and Robert Semple were perfectly sober, while Ezekiel Merritt and William Knight, who was serving as a semi-skilled translator, were nearly under the table. William Ide then came into the house, and the contrast of the busily scribbling and clearheaded Jacob Leese with the inebriated rebels caused him to later declare that the bottles had "vanquished the captors."

While the leaders inside Casa Grande continued their work, a larger group was still waiting in the Plaza. They were frustrated that the high drama they anticipated had fizzled into a gentlemanly exchange of documents. They had also started drinking some brandy brought out for their enjoyment by a Canadian resident. They started to talk about looting, and their shouts caught the attention of the men indoors, who rushed to the doorway of Vallejo's home. Semple threatened to shoot any man caught looting, and the nascent mob backed down, still muttering. Another resident offered them tea, and then some beef was prepared for their breakfast. They continued to grumble quietly among themselves, anxious to hear Ide's report from inside the house.

When the articles of surrender were finished, Vallejo signed the document, which included his pledge not to take up arms against the Americans. The rebels signed a separate declaration, also promising not to destroy property or injure anyone who did not oppose their ongoing efforts. Then, amazingly, Leese was released—or he released himself—and went back to his home on the southwest side of the Plaza.

At long last, Ide brought the "Articles of Capitulation" outside. The men, who had waited hours for good news, were outraged to see that General Vallejo, his brother Salvador, and the general's secretary, Victor Prudon, were not going to be arrested. A few began to ask what Frémont's orders were on the subject, but no one knew and no one had anything in writing. Some felt their principles had been betrayed, as they had all assumed the United States was behind their efforts. The crowd began to get ugly, and men started to talk again about looting Sonoma and then heading back to American territory. Ide was able to calm them down by declaring that they had all acted with honorable motives and that if they now acted dishonorably, they would forever be considered robbers instead of conquerors.

Leese, who returned to Casa Grande after eating breakfast, sensed that their surrender was not going to satisfy the majority of the angry rebels. His fears were confirmed when Semple told him that he, the Vallejos, and Prudon were being taken out of town under guard, and would be brought to Frémont himself. William Ide, who had the coolest head, elected to stay behind to keep order in Sonoma. A group of rebels commandeered horses and arms, and by noon the prisoners and their escort—led by Semple, Grigsby, and Merritt—put the pueblo behind them.

After a hard two-day ride, Vallejo, his brother, Prudon, and Leese were brought face-to-face with Frémont at his encampment on the American River. He did not give the Californios a satisfactory reason for their arrest, and he barely listened to their grievances, which included the loss of valuable livestock and supplies and the complete upending of order in Sonoma. After a short interview, Frémont collected some men and escorted his prisoners to Sutter's Fort. They were locked in an upstairs office for a while and later in an actual cell, both of which were too small and offered no comforts. There, they waited.

Meanwhile, the Californio men of Sonoma who were old enough to bear arms were being located and moved to the Plaza under guard. Everyone assumed that they would be combative and angry, but Ide and his cohorts were surprised to learn that most of them were in favor of an

American takeover (though they would have preferred one that did not roust them out of their homes). The rebels decided to release them, but to ensure that they wouldn't turn on the Americans, Ide made them adhere to a set of conditions under which they had to live for the duration.

Franklin Sears and Granville Swift convinced William Todd that their movement and their new republic needed a flag. Todd managed to obtain some unbleached cotton and deep red flannel. He sewed the red piece onto the bottom of the off-white cotton, and using "linseed oil and Venetian red or Spanish brown," according to an account he published in 1878, he wrote the words *California Republic* at the top. Above this he sketched a single star, which was a reference to the independent republic of Texas. Next to the star he drew a California grizzly bear, a symbol of strength and ferocity. As he worked, a breeze came up. Platón Vallejo, the general's five-year-old son, who had stepped out of the house to watch him work, held the flag down with his toe.

Todd was not prepared for the jeers that greeted his efforts. Both the Americans and the Californios thought the bear looked more like a pig. But the artwork didn't matter as much as the sentiment, and the flag was raised on the northeast side of the Plaza to the sound of cheers and toasts. From then on, the rebels would be known as the Bears or, in Spanish, Los Osos.

The following day Ide issued a proclamation outlining the reasons for the revolt. Perhaps unconsciously invoking the Declaration of Independence, Ide spelled out the reasons for the takeover, which included the shameful appropriation of mission property and interference with American commerce. He then invited "all peaceful & good citizens of California, who are friendly to the maintenance of good order and equal rights . . . to repair to my camp at Sonoma, without delay."

It seemed the Bear Flag Revolt would be calm and bloodless, a good start for a new political enterprise. But it didn't last.

On June 19, two young Bears named Thomas Cowie and George Fowler headed toward Santa Rosa on a scouting mission. They were captured by Mexican militiamen, tied to trees, beaten, and tortured. One of the torturers was a local man named "Three-fingered Jack" Garcia, a Sonoma barber and sometime horse thief. Cowie and Fowler were then killed and the murderers fled the area. The next day, other militia members took William Todd and an unidentified British subject hostage and held them at the site of a Miwok village called Olompali, south of Petaluma.

Frémont himself appeared in Sonoma on June 25, and used the death and capture of Americans to whip up the emotions of the Bear Flaggers who were still in town. He gathered a number of men, including Grigsby, Sears, Ford, and Swift. The last two led an attack on Olompali and rescued Todd, though the Englishman was killed. More skirmishes caused the deaths of many Californios.

Frémont, always ready to believe any rumor, then heard that Sonoma had been taken over by Mexican troops. So, on June 28, he directed his men back to town. Ide, who had remained in Sonoma, received reports of horsemen heading that way, so he readied the remaining Bears and mounted cannons aimed at the southern entrance to the valley. Famed mountain man Kit Carson, who had been with Frémont on many of his expeditions, was with him again and heard the Bears ready the cannons as he and the troop rode toward town. He yelled a warning to Frémont and his men and, luckily for everyone, Ide recognized Carson's voice and did not give the order to fire. Both groups rode together into town, and then Frémont's force headed south to their encampment in Sausalito.

Frémont returned to Sonoma for an Independence Day fiesta on July 4, and then decided to make himself the official commander of the collected Bears. He created a "California Battalion," with which he expected to control all activities of the revolt and decided to make his headquarters at Sutter's Fort. However, events in the United States were about to catch up with him and his California Republic.

On May 13, 1846, the United States had declared war on Mexico, and Commodore John D. Sloat, patrolling the seas off Mazatlán, headed to Monterey. On July 7 he sailed into the harbor, raised the American flag, and took the capital of Mexican California for America. Two days later, Captain John B. Montgomery did the same in Yerba Buena, raising the Stars and Stripes at today's Portsmouth Square, so named for Montgomery's ship.

That same day, July 9, Lieutenant Charles Warren Revere, grandson of Paul Revere, rode into Sonoma. It was his job to hoist the American flag on the Plaza, and as the Bear Flag came down, many of the remaining rebels in town complained about the end of their republic.

Most of the Californio residents were thrilled, however. It was the end of incompetent rule out of Monterey and Mexico City. And it was the beginning of what they hoped would be a peaceful, orderly, and prosperous time for newly American Sonoma. But the one man who could have rejoiced the most was still a prisoner: General Vallejo, along with his brother Salvador, and Jacob Leese, remained at Sutter's Fort, suffering in the summer heat. Not until August 2 were papers drawn up to release the general, and his companions wouldn't be freed until August 8.

Once back home, Vallejo was relieved to see that although he and the others had lost livestock and belongings during their absence (which irritated his brother more than it did him), their families had been protected. Chief Solano was partly responsible for this, and Ide did the rest. The Bears themselves were relieved that Vallejo did not use his influence to organize a resistance movement, not understanding that he supported their ideals, if not their actions.

As he recovered from his ordeal—he had been very ill and had lost a great deal of weight—Vallejo came to terms with the changes in town, even as he referred to June 1846 as the blackest month of his life. Soon after returning home, he made a gesture that marked the beginning of his life as a resident of the United States: He burned his Mexican uniform and shaved off his military beard. And on October 5 he traveled to Yerba

Edwin A. Sherman, Sonoma's first city clerk, made this sketch of the raising of the American flag after the Bear Flag Revolt. Courtesy Sonoma Valley Historical Society. Used by permission.

Buena to march in a parade to honor Commodore Robert F. Stockton, the commander of the American military forces stationed in California.

Vallejo's sister Rosalía Leese was not as forgiving. In an 1874 interview she railed against the Bears and the way they had treated her husband, herself, and their property during the weeks of the revolt. She referred to Frémont as a coward and called the rebels a "ring of thieves." To the end of her days, she refused to learn or speak English.

The war with Mexico raged in the West and California throughout 1846 and 1847. Troops were sent to California, and some ended up in Sonoma, which still had military importance. In April 1847 members of the First Regiment of New York Volunteers, also known as Stevenson's Regiment, arrived on the Plaza.

Colonel Jonathan D. Stevenson was a New York Democratic politician who had been recruited by Secretary of War William L. Marcy to gather a regiment to assist with US efforts in the Mexican-American War. He managed to recruit more than nine hundred young men but had only thirty-eight officers to manage them. The new soldiers were clerks, mechanics, and farmers, but also local toughs who simply liked a good fight. After they showed up in San Francisco, a large contingent was sent to southern California, but Company C, commanded by Captain John E. Brackett, was assigned to Sonoma. They were quartered in the old Mexican barracks, and a house one block east of the Plaza owned by John Ray—still there today—was their mess hall.

Commodore Stockton had created his own California Battalion of Mounted Riflemen, naming Frémont an officer. Los Angeles was the epicenter of the battle for California, and after losing the city more than once, General Stephen Watts Kearny and his force recaptured Los Angeles on January 10, 1847. On January 13, Governor Pío Pico surrendered to Frémont, and the war officially ended on February 2, 1848, with the signing of the Treaty of Guadalupe Hidalgo. California was now truly American.

IN LATER YEARS, many of the Bears would prosper, and some would lend their names to places around the Sonoma Valley.

William Ide fought in the Mexican War, returned to Sonoma, and was later a miner and a judge in Colusa County.

Granville Swift made a fortune in the Gold Rush and built Temelec Hall just a few miles from the Plaza, which was one of the most expensive homes in the county. It still stands today on the grounds of the Temelec retirement community.

Franklin Sears married Swift's sister, Margaret. Together the two men acquired thousands of acres of land near what is today called Sears Point, the site of Infineon Raceway.

Robert Semple went on to co-found California's first newspaper, the *Californian,* and occasionally used its columns for his own purposes. On August 14, 1847, he printed an article titled "Strayed or Stolen!!!" and asked for the return of a pair of silver mounted pistols with holsters, which had belonged to Jacob Leese. He said they were "well known by most of the volunteers under Frémont" and offered a ten-dollar reward for their recovery.

After the end of the Mexican War, Commodore Stockton made John Frémont California's military governor. He refused to obey the orders of the other top soldier in California, Stephen Watts Kearny, who had been given different instructions from Washington. Frémont was court-martialed, and though he was pardoned by President Polk, he decided to leave the army. He continued to write and undertake privately funded expeditions to California, where he acquired a large piece of property that later proved to contain rich veins of gold. A US senator and failed presidential candidate, he continued to act rashly throughout the Civil War years and lost his fortune through the mismanagement of his California holdings. His last years were spent drumming up support for railroads in the West and serving as territorial governor of Arizona.

When Stevenson's Regiment was disbanded in 1848 most of the soldiers left town, but a few stayed in Sonoma. Many of them became prominent citizens in town and beyond, such as John Cameron, Sonoma's first American mayor; Captain John Frisbie, who married one of General Vallejo's daughters and was later the secretary of the first California constitutional convention; and Thaddeus M. Leavenworth, the chaplain and alcalde of Yerba Buena, which was renamed San Francisco in January 1847. He later held property in nearby Boyes Springs.

As the nineteenth century went on, memories of the Bear Flag Revolt become romanticized, especially as California moved past its early

Nearly five thousand people converged on Sonoma in June 1896 to observe the fiftieth anniversary of the Bear Flag Revolt. Courtesy Sonoma Valley Historical Society. Used by permission.

statehood and into decades of growth and prosperity. On June 13, 1896, a celebration of the fiftieth anniversary of the Bear Flag Revolt was held in Sonoma, and nearly five thousand people turned out to see a parade and enjoy the festivities. Trains full of revelers brought people from San Francisco and Petaluma. Members of the Native Sons of the Golden West, the Grand Parlor of Native Daughters of the Golden West, and veterans of the Mexican War and the Civil War joined the parade. Of the original thirty-three Bears, only three were still alive, and only two were able to make it to the event.

And what of the Bear Flag itself?

When Lieutenant Revere replaced Todd's flag with the Stars and Stripes, he put the flag in his pocket and then gave it to John Elliott Montgomery, the son of Captain Montgomery, of Portsmouth Square (and Montgomery Street) fame in San Francisco. It traveled back east on the *Portsmouth* and was deposited with the Department of the Navy. In 1855 California senators John B. Weller and William M. Gwin asked Secretary of the Navy J. C. Dobbin to return the flag to California so it could be properly preserved for the citizens of the state. Dobbin was pleased to oblige, and on September 8, 1855, Senator Weller donated the flag to the Society of California Pioneers in San Francisco, founded in 1850 to preserve the records of early California. It was considered such a sacred relic that the society never loaned it out for displays, not even at the fiftieth anniversary commemorations in 1896. Instead, the society created replicas of the flag, though it's not clear if one was used at the Sonoma celebration.

The flag was displayed at Pioneer Hall until 1906, when it was destroyed, along with the society itself, in the firestorm that followed the great earthquake of April 18. In 1919 Sonoma County residents were riveted by the story that the original Bear Flag had been discovered in a Santa Rosa bank vault. It turned out to be one of the original replicas, which had been placed there in 1878, though no one remembered why.

In 1936 members of the Ancient and Honorable Order of E Clampus Vitus, a historical drinking society that erects plaques marking historic sites throughout the western states, convened at Sutter's Fort. A plaque was unveiled to mark the spot where James Marshall told John Sutter about the gold he discovered in 1848, which touched off the Gold Rush. The fort's curator, Henry C. Peterson, told the group that he was going to unveil a very important artifact, and started by telling a story.

On April 18, 1906, he was on San Francisco's Fourth Street near Market, and watched the fire approach the headquarters of the Society of California Pioneers. A guard let him walk into the building to take a final look before the place was blown up as a firebreak. The curators had taken many treasures with them, but had left a wrapped item behind. Peterson took the package, ran out of the building, and then shoved it under the seat of his automobile, where he forgot about it until it was discovered by one of his relatives.

As he now had the audience's attention, Peterson turned off the lights and then lit a lantern to illuminate something in his hands: the original Bear Flag. The "Clampers" rushed to take a look, exclaiming about the significance of the find. But it didn't take long for the experts among them to realize that Peterson's piece of fabric was a hoax, and he barely escaped being thrown into the Sacramento River.

In 1896 a Sonoma man named Alfred J. Puckett expressed the feelings of many in a poem he wrote for the Bear Flag's fiftieth anniversary celebration:

> We will give that flag protection
> In our love and warm affection
> For Pacific's pioneers,
> 'Tis to us a heart felt pleasure
> To preserve it as a treasure
> Through the long effacing years.

His sentiments were only partly shared by the Californios who remained in Sonoma as the territory headed toward statehood in 1850. As much as men like Vallejo had wanted the United States to take California, the result was bittersweet. Californio families lost much of their land in American courts, or saw their property overrun by the hordes who arrived to look for gold. Vallejo later rose to prominence as a legislator, but his holdings and his influence in town were never the same.

Sonoma didn't completely forget its roots in Latin America, though. Evidence of that early history can be seen every day, and from nearly every storefront.

Chapter Three

Sonoma's Historic Architecture

$\mathcal{S}$onoma's history is also written in brick, wood, and stone. The buildings around town that charm visitors today range from historic adobes to typically American stores and hotels, not to mention a former Carnegie library. As Sonoma made the transition from its days as a Mexican military outpost to its new life as an American city, the past was not completely discarded. Like revisionist history, the original buildings were put to new uses. As the decades passed, their original meaning and purpose were not necessarily forgotten, but the memory of their place in the city's history faded, awaiting a romantic revival that brought them back to life a century ago.

But even as more Americans moved into town during the Gold Rush and after California statehood in 1850, altering Sonoma's appearance forever, there was one architectural element that no one considered changing, except for the better: the heart of the city, the Plaza.

Plazas can be found all over the world, thanks to Roman and—in America—Spanish colonization. The word *plaza,* or *piazza* in Italian, derives from the Latin *platea,* from which we get the word *place,* and it originally meant a square or marketplace set off from a grid of streets. This function was formalized in 1573 by Philip II of Spain, when he issued a document called *Ordinances for the Discovery, New Settlement, and Pacification of the Indies,* later known as the Laws of the Indies. Plaza design was based on the urban planning style described in the most famous architectural manual of the classical world, *The Ten Books of Architecture*, by Vitruvius.

The Laws of the Indies were very specific about the way that sites in new regions were to be chosen. Future Spanish towns were supposed to have fertile land, preferably in an elevated area, and be close to a water source (something Father Altimira kept in mind when choosing the site for his mission).

When it was time to lay out the streets of a new pueblo, the city center —the plaza—was reserved first, and was meant to serve as pasturage and a place for recreation and public observances. In coastal towns, it was built where ships came in for landing, and in inland towns like Sonoma, it formed the center. Streets were supposed to radiate out from a plaza's corners like a star, but by the time Sonoma was being organized, a system of grids paralleling the plaza's sides was used instead. The *Ordinances* were still in effect, but were not strenuously enforced.

The Sonoma Plaza is not the oldest one in California. That distinction belongs to San José, whose central square was built in 1777. Los Angeles came next, in 1781. But Sonoma's was the largest in the state, and remains so to this day, eight acres in size.

When it was time to lay out the new city streets in 1835, General Vallejo brought William A. Richardson from Yerba Buena to help him do the survey. Richardson had already created the street plan in the growing village by the bay, and he was the perfect man for the job. Surveying and measuring the boundaries were probably performed in the traditional manner: riders on horseback used a specific length of rope to measure linear distances, placing a stick in the ground at intervals until the desired street length had been reached.

The mission was their starting point, and the men extended the short road in front of the church due west, past the large lot granted to Salvador Vallejo, along Calle Vallejo (now Spain Street). Eventually, all the streets were laid out, creating the open central area designated for the Plaza.

Today's First Street West was called either Salvador or Huerta Street, since it passed in front of one of Salvador Vallejo's properties where he happened to have an orchard. Napa Street, the main road to the namesake valley, was originally called United States Street. Broadway, the wide boulevard that intersects the Plaza and is the only street that doesn't parallel the square, was originally Calle Principal, or Main Street. The name was changed in the 1850s, reflecting Sonoma's more American character.

Although the Plaza today is an oasis of greenery, water, and graceful buildings, it was not always so. Edwin Bryant, the co-editor of Kentucky's *Louisville Courier* newspaper, made the trek to California in 1846 and was with John Frémont as he battled in Los Angeles during the Mexican War. In October 1846 he visited Sonoma, and described the Plaza this way: "Most of the buildings are erected around a *plaza*, about two hundred yards square. The only ornaments in this square are numerous skulls and dislocated skeletons of slaughtered beeves, with which hideous remains the ground is strewn."

Even by 1861, when a writer for the *California Farmer and Journal of Useful Sciences* published a short article about the square, things had not much improved. "We don't know of a prettier spot than the 'Plaza of Sonoma'—we mean, of course, when the citizens understand the duty they owe to their credit, and shall have it neatly fenced and planted with trees. The moment this is done, all the property *round the Plaza* will be worth one hundred per cent advance. Think of this, citizens of Sonoma!"

Increasing property value was important to the new and growing population of Americans in town. And as the years of Mexican rule fell away, more buildings were added "round the Plaza." But the city's original adobes still lived, and still served. The stories of a few of the most important will illustrate the fate and current condition of the many others that remain in town today.

THE ORIGINAL INDIAN VILLAGE OF HUCHI is long gone, overtaken by the construction of the mission. The small *ranchería* where some mission converts were allowed to live also disappeared from the city's face, its remnants surfacing only occasionally in the creek bed or in old backyard gardens in the form of arrowheads, beads, shells. But the mission and the barracks, built with Indian labor, still survive on their original sites.

The cluster of buildings that made up Mission San Francisco Solano was converted to new uses during the years of secularization. Eventually, many structures just disappeared. When Edwin Bryant visited in the autumn of 1846 he observed that "Sonoma is one of the old mission establishments of California; but there is now scarcely a mission building standing, most of them having fallen into shapeless masses of mud; and a few years will prostrate the roofless walls which are now standing."

The original adobe church crumbled so much that Vallejo ordered a new one built in 1840. It too was in a sorry state a few years later, and Vallejo made changes to the building to keep it intact, as it was the church where he and others worshipped on Sundays. In the late 1850s he arranged for a New England–style belfry to be constructed on the roof near the front. A decade later the facade of the church received a new facing of red brick. Other architectural details were altered in such a way that the original Spanish-style lines completely disappeared.

The old barracks fared a bit better. When members of the American military lived there after the Bear Flag Revolt, many of them called it "Camp Sonoma," a name that fortunately did not stick. Stevenson's Volunteers made a few improvements to the building during their time in town in 1847. They replaced damaged or missing roof tiles with redwood shingles and completed the second floor.

Two years later, General Persifer F. Smith, head of the Pacific Division of the US Army and governor general of occupied California, moved his troops into the barracks. He was famous enough to occasionally make the San Francisco papers. On January 31, 1850, the *Daily Alta California* reported that Smith had come into the city from his headquarters at Sonoma: "We are told that he comes down upon duties connected with his command, and will again return in the course of a few days." The article ended with: "We are pleased to hear that he is in excellent health." It's not clear whether this was just filler or if General Smith's health had been an issue in the past. In March, Smith went to San Francisco again, visiting the Presidio there. He made these visits regularly until 1852, when army headquarters were moved to the town of Benicia. After the military decamped, the barracks took on a very different life.

Once Smith's troops were out of the way, A. J. Cox moved in and started printing a newspaper called the *Sonoma Bulletin,* operating his business on the ground floor of the barracks. It lasted only until about

1855, when he moved to Vallejo to start another paper. But during those few years Cox made quite an impression on his fellow Sonomans, and he was even mentioned in other newspapers. In July 1853 an anonymous San Francisco reporter spent a few days in the area and wrote up his visit for the *Daily Alta California*. Editor Cox, he wrote, was always called "the Bulletin," and his paper was the "salt of the city." The composing room at the barracks on the day the reporter visited was filled with vegetables and grains, and the writer wondered if people paid for their papers with produce. Cox told him they were simply examples of the area's superior agricultural products.

Next to the barracks, looming over the Plaza and the entire valley, was General Vallejo's Casa Grande. It was erected in the middle of the block (today's Spain Street), between the barracks and Salvador Vallejo's home. Shaped like an L, it was partially completed and the family probably installed there by late 1836 (it was finished by 1840). This is where Vallejo was living on the morning of June 14, 1846, when the Bear Flaggers pounded on his massive front door.

Edwin Bryant visited Vallejo's house during his Sonoma excursion, and was astonished at the luxury and refinement he saw there.

General Valléjo is a native Californian, and a gentleman of intelligence and taste far superior to most of his countrymen. The interior of his house presented a different appearance from any house occupied by native Californians which I have entered since I have been in the country. Every apartment, even the main entrance-hall and corridors, were [*sic*] scrupulously clean, and presented an air of comfort which I have not elsewhere seen in California. The parlor was furnished with handsome chairs, sofas, mirrors, and tables, of mahogany framework, and a fine piano, the first I have seen in the country. Several paintings and some superior engravings ornamented the walls.

But Casa Grande wasn't just about domestic comfort. In 1843 the general erected a three-story, forty-foot tower, which was supposed to be used as an observatory. Given the political climate before the American takeover in 1846, it's easy to imagine what Vallejo hoped to observe from this grand perch.

His brother Salvador was also quite the property holder. He owned what was called the Post Commander's House, next door to Casa Grande. He first built a small home on the site in 1836 and then added an east wing in 1850. He obtained a lot on the west side of the Plaza along today's First Street West in 1843 as well, which he used for rental income.

Farther down this street was another adobe home, situated on the southwest corner of the Plaza, which belonged to Jacob Leese and his wife, Vallejo's sister Rosalía. They built the house in 1841 and had been living there for nearly five years when Leese was rousted from his bed by the Bears. By 1848 Leese was trying to make money selling merchandise brought over from China, and in 1849 he and his wife moved to Monterey. He sold the building to Vallejo, who then sold it to his sister-in-law, Josefa Carrillo Fitch, the widow of ship captain Henry Delano Fitch. Josefa didn't live in the house, but rented it to General Persifer Smith and his wife, who made it their home while the US Army occupied the barracks.

These quaint adobes were visited by men who heard about the charms of the Sonoma Valley and who also saw opportunity there. With the army in town, established farms nearby, and families moving slowly into the area, the place was ripe for business.

IN THE YEARS that followed the Bear Flag Revolt, Americans started commercial ventures in town and advertised them in a variety of San Francisco papers. In May 1847 W. W. Scott placed a notice in the *California Star,* informing readers that he had established a mercantile business in Sonoma and was prepared to "supply farmers and others with all articles usually kept in the stores of the country, at San Francisco retail prices." As an added incentive, Mr. Scott incorporated a bar into his store, which he kept stocked with choice wines and liquors.

In 1848 General Vallejo's former personal secretary Victor Prudon formed a partnership with an M. J. Haan to open a store offering a general assortment of dry goods, groceries, and so on. Another enterprise, the Morrow Store, was located at the corner of today's Napa and First Street East, and under new management has been a mercantile ever since. Even former Bear William B. Ide went into business, advertising his services as a surveyor, charging four dollars per mile for horizontal lines, one dollar for establishing corners and doing the paperwork for the "accustomary prices." He gave a 25 percent discount for cash.

One Sonoma resident wrote a letter to the *Californian* newspaper in March 1848 praising the improvements he had seen in the year since he had moved to town. Where once only shanties, unfinished cottages, and dilapidated adobes stood, now new dwellings had been built, and the town had seen a doubled population, improved streets, and the organization of a town council. "More business is now being transacted here than ever before and all branches of mechanical industry have had good encouragement," he wrote. Was he a local property owner or businessman hoping to entice more people to move to the area? We don't know, but he was about to see Sonoma's industry improve even more.

The Gold Rush of 1849, which changed the face of California forever and helped bring it into the Union the following year, had a profound effect on Sonoma. Lilburn Boggs, former Missouri governor, recent immigrant, and current Sonoma alcalde, actually got his hands on some gold dust in March 1848, only two months after James Marshall found the first glittering pieces at Sutter's Mill, and well before the discovery was nationally known. He had heard the wild stories coming out of Sacramento and visited Sutter at his fort to find out what was really going on. He also had a store in Sonoma, which he advertised in the *Californian* in both English and Spanish, offering "Dry Goods, Hardware, Groceries, and Tobacco," which he sold for either cash or hides. He realized early on what the gold discovery could mean for local merchants. And he was right.

Sonoma was one of the routes to the goldfields, and men stopped to rest, buy supplies, make necessary repairs to their vehicles, and check on their horses' shoes. Then, if they were lucky, these same voyagers stopped to spend some of their gold in Sonoma on their way back to San Francisco or points east.

By the early 1850s hotels began to open around the Plaza to serve visitors and—hopefully—future residents. One of the earliest that still survives is the Blue Wing Inn, located across from the mission, a few yards from the Plaza's northeast side. Its lot was originally granted in 1836 to Antonio Ortega, the majordomo of the mission during secularization.

Within a year Ortega was living in a small adobe on the site, and as late as 1848 he was still there, selling liquors out of a small shop.

In August 1849 he sold the building to Thomas Spriggs, an English ships' carpenter, and James Cooper, a transplanted Scot. They built a second story onto the original adobe and added a balcony, in the style of the adobes of Monterey. By 1852 a two-story addition had been built on the west side, and Spriggs and Cooper were operating the "Sonoma House." General Persifer's soldiers were frequent guests, as the place was a gambling house and saloon, in addition to being a hotel. By 1853 the name had changed to Blue Wing Inn, and there was another Sonoma House elsewhere in town.

There is some evidence to suggest that Cooper operated another local establishment called the Occidental Hotel in 1848, before buying the Sonoma House with Spriggs the following year. General Vallejo was apparently one of his customers, and records show that he was a light drinker but did enjoy frequent games of billiards.

The Union Hotel and Hall opened for business in 1849, near the corner of today's Napa Street and First Street West. Three Mexican war veterans built the one-story adobe hotel and wood-framed hall, and it was receiving rave reviews within a decade. It set a good table, had good sleeping arrangements, and offered clean linens.

The Swiss Hotel, still operating on the Plaza today, was originally part of Salvador Vallejo's home next to his brother's Casa Grande. In the 1870s it was possibly used as a stage stop, but didn't become a hotel until it was taken over by the Torino family in 1892. When another hotel across the Plaza burned down, the Torino family took its name for their own place: the Swiss Hotel.

A few yards east of the Swiss is the Toscano Hotel, the oldest commercial wood-frame building in town. It didn't start out as a hotel, however. Built in 1851, it originally housed a retail store and rental library called Nathanson's. It became the Eureka Hotel after that business, located on East Napa Street and Broadway, burned down in 1877 (renaming hotels for their burned-out predecessors seems to have been a local tradition). By 1886 the building's Italian owners renamed it the Toscano: the Tuscan.

Today's Sonoma Hotel started life as Weyl Hall in 1879, a grocery store and dance hall combination. It was converted to a hotel in the 1920s.

The El Dorado Hotel, another Plaza survivor, started out as part of Salvador Vallejo's rental empire in the late 1840s. In 1851 the northern portion of his adobe structure became the El Dorado, managed by two former members of Stevenson's Regiment, Isaac Randolph and George Pearce. They added a frame second story to the building, and then in March 1852 they sold the lower floor to a group of men for a Masonic hall. Unpaid mortgages forced the sale of the buildings, and from 1858 to 1866 the Cumberland Presbyterian Literary College for Young Ladies and Gentlemen was in residence.

These young ladies and gentlemen had no local newspaper to read to help them with their literary endeavors. The *Californian,* a San Francisco paper, was distributed in town as early as 1847, with General Vallejo holding the delivery franchise. But there was a dearth of neighborhood news. The *Sonoma Bulletin* lived for only a few years after its startup in 1852, and after it closed in 1855 Sonoma was without a newspaper until April 17, 1879, when the *Sonoma Index* put out its first issue. Renamed the *Sonoma Index-Tribune* in 1884, it has been published continuously ever since.

Sonoma's original commercial ventures—mercantiles selling dry goods, tobacco, etc.—continued to thrive as the Gold Rush years passed into and through the Civil War era.

Solomon Schocken, owner of what came to be known as the Schocken

TOP: The Schocken store in the remodeled barracks building, 1880s. Courtesy Sonoma Valley Historical Society. Used by permission.

BOTTOM: Julius and Catherine Poppe's son Charles opened his own store in Glen Ellen, pictured here in 1883. Courtesy Sonoma Valley Historical Society. Used by permission.

store, was one of the most well known of the city's entrepreneurs. He arrived in Sonoma in 1873, and by 1878 he owned the former barracks building, converting the eastern portion into his general store. The other side was made into apartments, and he later gave the entire structure a gaudy Victorian facade. Anyone looking at photos taken of the building and its surroundings at the end of the nineteenth century, or visiting the building in person, would never have guessed that the Schocken store was once a Mexican military stronghold. He began to advertise heavily in the 1870s, touting his new store—the barracks—on the northeast corner of the Plaza.

In 1881 Schocken purchased the remaining mission buildings, which had been put up for sale by the diocese in order to build a new church for the growing Sonoma parish. For $3,000 (about $67,000 today) Schocken bought the chapel, the padres' house next door and the land behind it. In 1889, while excavating for a 60,000-gallon water tank on the property, his workmen struck a brick pavement two feet below the surface. The bricks were twelve inches square and were laid out in tidy rows on a layer of sand and gravel. No one knows today exactly where this pavement was found, as it was soon covered up. A writer for the *Sonoma Index-Tribune* speculated that it might have been the floor of one of the original mission buildings.

Julius A. Poppe, originally from Germany, had a general store on the Plaza beginning in 1860, which was run by his wife, Catherine, after his death in 1880. But he was more famous in town for his unusual side business: carp breeding. He imported German carp to Sonoma in 1874, and over the next few years he made quite a good living selling his fish to local and national markets. He had a number of spring-fed rearing ponds at the former ranchería called Pulpuli, on Highway 121 where Cline Cellars is today.

Another big businessman was A. F. Pauli, whose eponymous business was located on the south side of the Plaza. He offered both staple and fancy groceries, confectionery, "Gents' Furnishing Goods," and "Lakeshore Yeast Powder," which was famous enough to warrant big letters in the display ads he placed in the *Sonoma Index-Tribune* in the 1880s. Not only that—there was apparently a prize in every can.

And of course there were plenty of saloons in town, which catered to

American tastes in intoxicating spirits: the Pioneer Saloon, A. J. Hubsch's Saloon, M. Powell's New Saloon, Monahan's Wine Rooms, to name a few. The better hotels like the Union and the Blue Wing also had well-stocked bars.

General Vallejo didn't think much of the drinks served around town. A winemaker himself, as well as a brandy distiller, he was used to drinking spirits made with care and with local ingredients. But, as he wrote in his memoirs, "before the coming of Frémont, we drank only pure liquor, and that in small quantities, and everyone enjoyed good health, tenacious memories, and lively intelligence." Once the Americans started importing hard liquors from France and Germany, made with chemicals and "noxious herbs," diseases of the nervous system began to take hold of Sonoma's young men, clouding their minds and undermining their constitutions. But the general's opinion did not stem the rising tide of liquor sales; that was left to Prohibition a few decades later.

New buildings going up around Sonoma in the 1850s tended to be constructed in a more American style than the city's original structures from the Mexican era. Residents transplanted from the Midwest and New England created their commercial buildings and homes with multi-paned windows, crown molding, and other less indigenous features. They rarely used adobe. Adobe meant the past, and even though it was often used as insulation (for which it was eminently suited), it hardly ever showed up on a building's exterior.

One home that perfectly reflected the era's architectural styles was built, not surprisingly, by General Vallejo. Between 1851 and 1852 Vallejo erected a trendy, Gothic-style mansion a few blocks west of Casa Grande and named it Lachryma Montis, or "Tears of the Mountain." Constructed beside and named for the spring called Chiucuyem—one of the selling points of the site—the home eventually expanded to multiple structures. A reservoir was built nearby to collect water, which was then run through redwood pipes and irrigated his crops and gardens, as well as supplying the needs of the house. Visitors to Lachryma Montis were impressed by the extensive vineyards and orchards that surrounded the house.

Vallejo rented out Casa Grande in 1853 to St. Mary's Academy, a young women's boarding school, where he also sent two of his daughters.

It closed three years later and was turned into a collection of apartments and offices. Then, on April 13, 1867, a fire roared through the building, utterly destroying it. It was a miracle that Nathanson's next door, the nearby barracks, and Salvador's home all escaped destruction. The general's wife, Benicia, wrote a sad letter to one of her daughters about coming to the Plaza to watch her home of fifteen years burn to the ground. Her husband and his brother could not bear to join her.

AS BUSINESSES IN TOWN began to prosper, local merchants decided that something had to be done about the Plaza. More people were coming to Sonoma to live, not just pass through, and these future customers were not impressed with the weed-strewn and ragged central square. The Plaza was important to these merchants, whose advertisements in local and regional papers often listed their addresses simply as "East Side of Plaza" or "United States St., Opposite Plaza." Cox's *Sonoma Bulletin* printed editorials about the need to fix up the Plaza, and in 1851 the city council appropriated $1,500 to level and improve the area. General Vallejo was on the committee charged with the Plaza upgrade, which proceeded in fits and starts over the next few decades.

By 1871 a picket fence surrounded the area, and in 1876 a man named Orick Johnson was allowed to keep cattle on the site in return for maintaining the grass grown there, but the cattle were gone by 1885. Residents had been in the habit of throwing excess lumber and wood scraps into the Plaza, and in October 1878 the city council ordered that all of this detritus be removed. In 1879 the Sonoma Valley Railroad Company built a depot, turntable, car barn, water tower, repair shed, and engine house on the northern section of the Plaza, near Spain Street. The rail complex dominated the Plaza for more than a decade.

An open-air pavilion was built in the fall of 1880 and then enclosed in 1886, serving for a time as the city hall. A bell was installed in its belfry, and in addition to rallying local volunteer firemen, it tolled to mark the assassination of President William McKinley in 1901. In 1885 the lack of lighting in the area prompted the *Sonoma Index-Tribune* to suggest that "City Dads" install streetlamps around the Plaza, "as we are liable to lose some of our best citizens one of these dark nights."

By 1887 it was obvious that the Plaza needed more work than the city could afford, so the Clay Literary Society held a benefit, and the following year $150 was appropriated for improvements. The money was mostly spent on trees and the laying of water pipes, which was what most people wanted for the Plaza, referred to in print as "forlorn" and "neglected."

The pavilion, which had originally been rejected by the city, proved to be useful for a few years. In 1888 it housed an exhibit of Sonoma Valley

The Plaza pavilion when it served as city hall, 1880s. Courtesy Sonoma Valley Historical Society. Used by permission.

products, and the local band also practiced there. More money was soon allocated to upgrade the fence, establish walkways, and make other improvements.

As the twentieth century loomed, the city realized that the Plaza could become more than just a fenced former cow yard, and structures and monuments more suited to a park soon began to appear within its borders.

The Sonoma Women's Club, formed in 1901, took up the challenge of beautifying the Plaza. The Plaza Fund was created, which included a $25 donation from Mrs. Phoebe Hearst, mother of publisher William Randolph Hearst and a famous Bay Area philanthropist (in today's dollars, her donation equaled about $650). By 1905 the Women's Club had collected the $230 needed to install a fountain at the southern edge of the Plaza where it meets Broadway. The women thought of

The Bear Flag Monument erected by the Native Sons of the Golden West in 1914. Collection of the author.

everything: there was a spigot for humans, dogs, and horses, and the fountain remained in place until 1932. In 1907 the club erected a stone monument to the memory of the Bear Flag Revolt, and it survives today on the northeast corner of the Plaza. A larger and more elaborate monument was put up by the Native Sons of the Golden West in 1914, just a few feet away.

As early as 1902 the city began to set aside money for a much-needed new city hall. The old Plaza pavilion just wasn't adequate, and by the spring of 1906 it looked as though the project would move forward as planned. Nature had something to say first, however.

Just before dawn on April 18, the massive San Francisco earthquake shook Sonomans out of their beds. Although many buildings sustained major damage, the town suffered no casualties, a fate that did befall the county seat in Santa Rosa, which lay in the path of the fault. Tents were erected in the Plaza to house refugees from other Bay Area cities, and the Women's Club collected donations of food and clothing. The braver souls in town trekked to nearby hilltops at night where they could see the crimson glow of the fires that were destroying the heart of San Francisco.

But repairs to buildings and nervous systems came quickly, and in

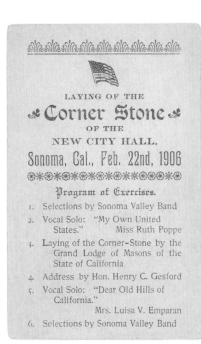

Official program for the laying of the city hall cornerstone, 1906. Collection of the author.

1907 contractors were invited to submit bids to build the city hall. Adolph Lutgens of San Francisco, whose brother, Henry, was a local Sonoma businessman, was the architect chosen to create the design. Henry's wife was also a member of the Women's Club and very involved with the creation of the Plaza fountain. Adolph visited his family regularly and was well known around town, so he was the logical choice for a group of people who had probably never had the occasion to engage an architect before.

In 1908 a local farmer paid $100 for the nearly thirty-year-old wooden pavilion, and used its wood to build a barn. And on California Admission Day, September 9, 1908, the new city hall was dedicated. It was built facing Broadway behind the Women's Club fountain on the south side of the Plaza. Locally quarried stone was used in its construction, and its four sides are identical, allegedly to present the same face to businesses at all points of the Plaza.

A couple of weeks after the city hall was dedicated, the Native Sons started a fund-raising campaign for more Plaza improvements and restoration. Once the new buildings were in place, and immature trees began to grow, the city council and other prominent citizens realized what a treasure the Plaza was and how much more it could serve the city. In May 1909 the Women's Club declared a "Sonoma Day," and a large plot of land in front of the city hall was reworked and filled with soil for the installation of a lawn. Another fountain, for the north side, was also planned by the local ladies.

Something else was missing in the new and improved Plaza, however: a library. So in February 1911 the city trustees decided to apply to Andrew Carnegie for the $6,000 needed to build a suitable structure. The magnate and philanthropist had been helping cities worldwide build new libraries since 1881, and Sonoma sent in photographs, exhibits, and local data to bolster its case. The answer came in July: the money was approved, and architect Adolph Lutgens was pressed into service again.

While plans were being drawn, the city was confronted with another, more local disaster, which could have made the plans come to an abrupt halt.

On September 23, a coal oil stove exploded in the kitchen of a cobbler shop on First Street East, just across the street from where the new library was to be built. Nearly all of the businesses on the block were obliterated, and the value of the loss amounted to almost $40,000 (nearly $1 million in today's dollars). A stiff wind hampered the efforts of dozens of firefighters, and just as they thought the blaze was under control, the wind shifted, sending the flames northward. In their path was the wine cellar of Agostino Pinelli and the Blue Wing Inn, which he also owned, and where he stored thousands of gallons of wine. Thinking quickly, he had the firemen haul their pumper to the Blue Wing, where they hooked the hose up to a storage tank. Within minutes a ruby stream was pouring out and dousing the flames, saving not only Pinelli's business but others nearby. The air smelled of wine for days.

Burned-out merchants didn't waste any time getting their stores up and running again, though for some it took longer to rebuild both buildings and stock. On February 17, 1912, Mrs. Catherine Poppe, who lost the popular Poppe store to the fire, placed an ad in the *Sonoma Index-Tribune* saying that she had moved her business to an adobe three doors from First Street West (the other side of the Plaza), "where she will carry

The Carnegie Library, now the Sonoma Valley Visitors Bureau. Collection of the author.

on a store similar to the one destroyed by the fire last September." The following year the new library opened, and as the decades progressed, the increasingly tree-filled square became the kind of place where Sonomans got together for celebrations, solemn observances, and just to enjoy the beautiful weather.

AT THE TURN OF THE TWENTIETH CENTURY, as local citizens were improving the look and usefulness of the Plaza, many of these same people also began to think about the buildings that lined its streets. They weren't too pleased with what they saw. The old adobe landmarks were disappearing, and many thought the remaining ones were hideous eyesores. There was a lot of talk about tearing them down.

While some residents wanted to modernize Sonoma and sweep away the adobes that marked its history, others were just as eager to preserve them. In 1895 writer Charles Fletcher Lummis had started a movement to restore California's missions and other historic remnants of its Hispanic past in the southern part of the state. He had recently taken over a tired Chamber of Commerce magazine called *Land of Sunshine* and turned it into a promotional publication to advertise California's romantic past and entice visitors to come and view the historic remnants for themselves. He promoted the missions as the singular image of a past that was just past enough to be interesting. Their ruins were now picturesque instead of eyesores, and by 1902 a group called the Landmarks Club had

Mission San Francisco Solano in the 1910s. Collection of the author.

been formed to raise money to restore as many of California's missions as possible.

By 1903 this movement had gained traction in Sonoma. In May the *Sonoma Index-Tribune* announced that William Randolph Hearst, publisher of the *San Francisco Examiner,* had donated $500 to a subscription list called the Landmarks Fund to help restore California's historic buildings. His paper also handled the publicity for the campaign. Invoking the value of the Alamo to the state of Texas, local enthusiasts pushed for the preservation of the mission buildings on the Plaza so that they could receive their "due homage" from the present generation. But it wasn't all about romantic associations with the past. Business owners also knew that fixing up the mission would attract tourists, many of whom made special trips to visit historic ruins. They threw their energy behind the campaign, and the Woman's Club and the Young Men's Institute joined in.

By the summer of 1903 the Landmarks Fund totaled $13,000 and Hearst was its trustee. Solomon Schocken was persuaded to sell the chapel, the padres' house, and its surrounding acreage in July for $3,000, which was what he had paid for it back in 1881, though its value by this time was about $72,000 in today's dollars. Work on the structures began immediately, and late-nineteenth-century additions were stripped away to reveal the mission's original lines. Money trickled in slowly, and the work proceeded the same way, but the project got a boost in 1906 when Hearst deeded the buildings and property to the State of California, which would organize its state park system twenty years later.

Surprisingly, the 1906 earthquake did little damage to the mission, though it did further weaken walls that were already a bit wobbly. But the hit-or-miss progression of restoration meant that the buildings were not systematically strengthened, and in 1909 the front half and southwest corner of the chapel collapsed after a year of heavy rains. A caretaker, paid for by the state, did his best to look after the structures, but it wasn't enough.

Luckily, the California Legislature appropriated enough money between 1911 and 1913 to finish the restoration work and get Mission San Francisco Solano ready to receive tourists. The chapel was opened to the public on June 14, 1914 (not coincidentally, the anniversary of the Bear Flag Revolt). There was also a small museum with a display of historical items for visitors to enjoy. In addition, the mission's second-oldest original bell, which dated to 1829 and which had been lost when the buildings were sold to Schocken, eventually turned up in the museum of the Sutro Baths in San Francisco. (The first bell, brought by William Richardson in 1825 and also lost, was never located.) The great bell was given back to Sonoma, thanks to the efforts of the Woman's Club, and restored to the beam outside the chapel, where it still resides today.

The city held a joyous Mission Centennial on the Plaza from June 30 to July 4, 1923, and locals dressed in historic costume turned out to attend the various events. It was a reason to celebrate not only the mission's rescue but the whole of Sonoma's history. California state senator Herbert Slater, a big supporter of the restoration efforts, said in a statement to the local paper about the importance of the Centennial: "There is no doubt but that this event can be made to stand out as a crowning glory of pageantry in California." Three years later, Mission San Francisco Solano was designated California Historical Monument Number 3, and its life as Sonoma's preeminent historical treasure began.

But it wasn't the only historical treasure in town. In the 1930s restoration efforts got under way at the barracks, still owned by veteran merchant Solomon Schocken. In 1935 he sold the building to Walter and Celeste Murphy, the publishers of the *Sonoma Index-Tribune,* and they renovated the structure for use as their residence, as well as offices. They

Sonoma's past and present are reflected in this photograph from the 1923 Mission Centennial. Courtesy Sonoma Valley Historical Society. Used by permission.

sold the building to the State of California in 1958 and lived there for the rest of their lives. As the century progressed, more buildings were designated California Historic Landmarks: General Vallejo's home, Lachryma Montis (#4), the Blue Wing Inn (#17), the Barracks (#316), the Swiss Hotel (#496), and the Salvador Vallejo adobe on First Street West (#501).

The Plaza also got a face-lift. The Mission Centennial of 1923 had made Sonoma's citizens prouder of their city, and the increased tourism made them more aware of how the Plaza looked to outsiders, much as it had done forty years earlier. A planned tax to help renovate the Plaza was soundly defeated, however, and private enterprise again took up the cause of Plaza beautification. In the 1930s plans for a children's playground, amphitheater, miniature lakes, and additional tree plantings were on the drawing board, and much of what is seen on the Plaza today resulted from these efforts, undertaken more than seventy-five years ago.

During World War II the Plaza was the site of many war bond drives. In June 1945, just weeks after Germany's surrender, a drive was held to aid the country in defeating the Japanese. Named "Army Day," it had a special attraction just for the local children. As people walked toward the Plaza that morning, past patriotic and historical displays in the windows of nearby businesses, they noticed something very large on the site. It was an M8 Scout Car, the heavily armored vehicle used by British and American troops in Europe and Asia, complete with a gun turret. Every time a bond was sold, a child was taken for a spin in the M8. A local man named Paul Wolter bought several bonds to give as many kids as possible the chance to take the ride of their life.

In 1951 Temple Lodge No. 14, the local Masonic lodge chartered in 1851, held its centennial on the Plaza. War protests in the 1960s replaced the war bond drives of the previous generation, as the Plaza became the site for gatherings of all kinds. Trees were planted, and ducks were installed in the artificial lake as the decades passed, making the square the obvious venue for everything from a vintage festival to today's farmers' markets. In 1991 the first "Red and White Ball" was held on the Plaza. In the grand tradition of historic Plaza improvement efforts, the ball was originally organized to improve the lighting on the square. It is now a much-anticipated event every summer, and the money raised benefits both the Plaza and local nonprofits.

Businesses and other enterprises have come and gone since the Plaza was a cow pasture and the mission was Sonoma's spiritual focal point. Many of the buildings constructed at the end of the nineteenth century or the beginning of the twentieth still surround the Plaza today: the Batto Building, the Temple Lodge, and the Leese-Fitch Adobe on the west side; Simmons Pharmacy, Hotz and Buccoli buildings on the south; the Duhring Building (rebuilt after a 1990 fire), Sebastiani Theatre, and Ice House on the east; and the original historic structures on the north side.

Time has changed the way these buildings function. Stores that once sold bolts of cloth or pickles and nails out of barrels now serve ice cream or sell fine home accessories. Drugstores have become clothing stores, and former hardware emporiums now host wine tastings. Each generation finds a way to bring new life to these historic structures, but their essence is always Sonoma.

Chapter Four

A Vine Tradition

On June 6, 1863, the "Married" column of the San Francisco *Daily Alta California* newspaper carried a brief announcement of a double wedding ceremony that took place in Sonoma on the first of the month. In two short paragraphs readers learned that Natalia and Jovita Vallejo, daughters of General M. G. Vallejo, had married A. F. and Arpad Haraszthy, respectively, and that the ceremony was observed at the home of the brides.

The kind of people who read marriage announcements in San Francisco's most important paper were very aware of who General M. G. Vallejo was. During the nearly twenty years since the Bear Flag Revolt, Vallejo had become a well-known and respected landowner and state legislator, venerated for literally putting Sonoma on the map. And though his name was not mentioned, most Bay Area readers also knew who the father of A. F. and Arpad Haraszthy was. Especially if they were wine drinkers. For Agoston Haraszthy was not just the father of the grooms. He was (and is) also considered by many to be the father of California wine.

The wedding was therefore more than just the joining of two families. It symbolized the blending of the two strands of history for which Sonoma is still known today. One is the city's origins in the crucible of Spanish and Mexican expansion, symbolized by the general himself. The other is Sonoma's storied wine industry, which owes much to Haraszthy's marketing genius. Without these two men, winemaking in the Valley of the Moon might never have happened.

IT STARTS, of course, with the grapes.

When Spanish missionaries arrived in California, they built churches and living quarters for themselves and the native peoples they hoped to convert. They also needed to grow food, and it was just as important to cultivate grapes to make wine, both for the sacrament of the Mass and for the table. These men came to their posts via Spain and Mexico, where they had learned the rudiments of winemaking, an essential skill for any missionary.

The padres at the southern California missions were the first to plant vineyards, though they did find wild grapes growing all over the region. Today these varieties are known as either *Vitis californica* or *Vitis girdiana;* the former is found in the northern part of the state, the latter in the south. However, no one knows if the missionaries tried to use this fruit to make wine. If they did, the results must have been unsatisfactory, if not undrinkable, because it seems that the padres wanted to grow grapes—instead of gather them—fairly soon after their arrival.

The first non-native vines planted in California were probably those at Mission San Juan Capistrano, brought there by a supply ship from Mexico in May 1778. The premier vintages were made around 1782, and vineyards were soon installed at missions from San Diego to San Francisco.

While waiting for the vines to mature, the missionaries had to import wine from missions in Baja California. This was a source of annoyance to everyone in the area. Even Father Junípero Serra vented his irritation in a letter to fellow Father Fermín Lasuén, saying that the lack of wine for the Mass was becoming "unbearable."

So what did the padres actually plant? Today the variety is called the Mission grape, but it originated in Spain, where it went by a number of names. Juice from this grape variety made a rather sweet, low-acid wine, and it was sometimes fortified with brandy to make a golden dessert cordial called Angelica. Served at table, the wine got mixed reviews, depending on the taste of the drinker.

When Father José Altimira founded Mission San Francisco Solano in 1823, planting grapes was one of his priorities. In the annual report to his superiors written at the end of 1824, he stated that there were one thousand grapevines in the ground, in a patch about three hundred yards east of the mission buildings. His vines probably came from cuttings taken at Mission San José, founded south of San Francisco in 1797. The hot, dry climate there was perfect for grapes. San Francisco's Mission Dolores was a lot closer to Sonoma and also had grapes on its lands, but they didn't do well in the city's infamous fog and wind. The padres tried making wine at Dolores, but the quality was deemed "ordinary."

Viniculture at the missions involved a lot of native labor—everything from tending the grapes to preparing them for fermentation. When it was time to harvest, the grapes were picked and typically placed on a platform covered with clean hides. A native convert then stomped around to get the grapes off the stems (there were probably other methods, but the literature on mission winemaking is a bit sparse). The juice that ran off the hides was caught in leather or rawhide bags, then fermented either in these bags or in a wooden tub, with or without the skins. Pressing and storage then took place, and some juice was reserved for brandy.

By 1833 the vineyard at the Sonoma mission was about two hundred square yards in size, surrounded by a stone and tile wall. A caretaker lived in a small adobe, water from a nearby spring fed the vineyard, and a good supply of wine filled the cellar. Then, when General Vallejo was ordered to secularize the mission that same year, he took a detailed inventory of the structures and grounds, mentioning the vineyard specifically. This wasn't just because he was an orderly military man. He was also a wine enthusiast. But famous as he was, the general was not the man who would make the city synonymous with fine wine. That distinction was to belong to a big-thinking Hungarian immigrant named Agoston Haraszthy.

HARASZTHY IS WELL KNOWN in Sonoma, and many people think that his fame rests solely in his achievement of bringing the city's winemaking into the modern era. But when he rolled into the valley in 1856, he already had a number of other accomplishments under his belt, including the distinctions of being the first Hungarian to settle in the

United States and serving as the first town marshal, county sheriff, and state assembly representative for the city of San Diego. He was also the first assayer at the US Mint in San Francisco.

Hungary had a grand winemaking tradition, and Haraszthy wanted to re-create it in his new homeland. After visiting the San Francisco Bay Area in 1852, he bought some property near San Francisco's Mission Dolores. But, as the missionaries had discovered, it wasn't the right place for wine grapes. In 1853 he relocated south of the city, and although wine was on his mind, he took the job of assayer for the US Mint in 1854. Haraszthy left there under a cloud three years later, suspected of improprieties that included the mysterious disappearance of gold dust, which escaped from the mint's chimneys and ended up on city rooftops. Though he was later exonerated, the experience helped him make the decision to turn his efforts again to winemaking.

Even as he worked at the Mint, Haraszthy kept looking for prime grape-growing land. He visited Sonoma in 1856, and the following year purchased a plot called Rancho Lac, or Vineyard Farm, which had had a string of owners since its origins as a land grant in 1842. When Haraszthy acquired the 176 acres, located about two miles from the Sonoma Plaza, a sizable vineyard was included, and he also purchased another 496 acres nearby. Even before he signed the papers making the property his own, Haraszthy named it Buena Vista, and he moved his family into the farmhouse built by one of the previous owners.

Vineyard Farm already had a press house, a brandy distillery, and 15,000 grapevines. With this situation as his starting point, Haraszthy planned to transform Buena Vista into California's most modern winemaking operation. He started out in the fall of 1857 by digging cellars into the cool hills. In the next year he expanded these for champagne storage and started the foundation for his new home, an Italian-style villa that was completed in 1860.

He surprised valley residents in 1859 by bringing a hundred Chinese men to Buena Vista to work in the vineyards, expand the existing cellars, and build structures for pressing and fermentation. They lived and worked in the area for ten years despite discrimination that sometimes threatened to break out into violence. Haraszthy championed the Chinese and did what he could to thwart not only local sentiment but

Chinese workers in the Sonoma Valley, from *Frank Leslie's Illustrated Newspaper*, December 25, 1880. Collection of the author.

also discriminatory laws. In September 1859 wines made by these field workers won numerous awards, vindicating Haraszthy's continued statements that the Chinese were good for California agriculture.

Word of the fine wines being made at Buena Vista traveled beyond Sonoma and the greater Bay Area. In 1860 a western survey expedition under the command of engineer Frederick William Lander stopped for Fourth of July celebrations in Mud Springs, Utah Territory. As he wrote in a letter to the *Daily Alta California,* he had managed to secure a small assortment of wines and liquors, among them, "a box of rich, red Sonoma wine, as pure as when it was first pressed from the blushing grapes of Buena Vista."

A year after this festive event, Haraszthy made a tour of Europe to observe winemaking techniques and ship European grapevines back to Sonoma. He intended to use these natives from across the pond to improve on the grape stocks he already had in his vineyards. In 1862 he published *Grape Culture, Wines, and Wine-Making,* generally acknowledged to be the first book ever published about California wine.

But by 1863 Buena Vista was in financial trouble. To get out of his predicament, Haraszthy decided to incorporate as the Buena Vista

Vinicultural Society (BVVS). Famous names such as San Francisco financier William Ralston and landscape architect Frederick Law Olmsted were among the stockholders. For a while, the winery's fortunes seemed to improve. Its "Sparkling Sonoma" received an honorable mention at the Universal Exposition in Paris in 1867. The leftover wine was then given to Louis Pasteur for his experiments on microbes and their effect on wine.

But it wasn't enough. Haraszthy filed for bankruptcy, and in 1868 he left Sonoma with family members, making his way to Nicaragua. He had an idea that products from this lush Central American country would go over well in California. The following year, he disappeared while traveling alone by a river near his home. No one knows whether he drowned or was dragged to his death by an alligator, but a mysterious demise seems a fitting end for this larger-than-life character.

Meanwhile, the BVVS managed to keep the winery in business. In 1872 the farm and ranch paper *Pacific Rural Press* printed an extensive article about Buena Vista, emphasizing the size of the vineyards and the volume of wine produced: 6,000 acres of vines and 230,000 gallons in the cellar. The article also mentioned the visit of San Francisco photographer Eadweard Muybridge, who took stereograph photos at Buena Vista throughout 1872.

Bottling at the Buena Vista Winery, 1870s. Courtesy Sonoma Valley Historical Society. Used by permission.

The Buena Vista "castle," 1920s. Collection of the author.

These images were printed in duplicate on one piece of card stock, then viewed in a special holder for a three-dimensional effect. Muybridge took a series of shots titled *A Vintage in California,* documenting nearly every aspect of the winemaking process: a man hand-cranking a crusher, workers fertilizing the vineyards at dawn, and many more.

But despite hard work and good publicity, Buena Vista's grandeur slowly faded. In 1880 the BVVS sold the winery and the vineyards at auction to Robert Johnson. He and his wife, Kate, built a grand castle on the site (Castle Road is named for the gaudy structure). In 1920 the State of California acquired the property, including the castle, and turned it into a home for "delinquent" women, who were probably responsible for burning it down in 1923. Another structure was built in its place, but Buena Vista's glory years disappeared from local memory.

Today, Haraszthy is often called the father of the California wine industry. This is sometimes interpreted to mean that he founded the first winery, or planted the first vineyards, but neither of these accolades is true. Commercial wineries and thriving vineyards existed in California before Haraszthy arrived, including in neighboring Napa Valley. Napa's wine industry dates to the 1860s, and early on it proved to be a formidable rival for the affections of wine drinkers.

But what Haraszthy did achieve was to recognize Sonoma's enormous potential as a winemaking region. By expanding his vineyards with European vines, writing and lecturing about local vintages, and presiding over a variety of vinicultural organizations, he spread the word about Sonoma in ways that had never been done before. As early as the 1850s, even as the rest of the world rushed to California to find gold, Haraszthy saw Sonoma's fortunes growing on sun-dappled vines.

HARASZTHY wasn't the only winemaker in town. General Vallejo was managing vineyards before Sonoma was established as a pueblo. According to Vallejo family lore, he transplanted vines from the mission lands to his own property after secularization. When the governor-general of the Hudson's Bay Company, Sir George Simpson, paid a visit to Sonoma in 1841, he tasted some of Vallejo's wines, and later wrote that he had 540 gallons in his cellar. By 1860 Vallejo had 4,000 bearing grapevines and 10,000 cuttings, and he made 8,000 gallons of wine.

His cellars were located in the old barracks on the Plaza. P. A. Giovanini supervised his vineyards, and Dr. Victor J. Faure lived at the barracks and was in charge of the actual winemaking. Vallejo displayed his vintages at fairs in Petaluma, Marysville, San Francisco, and Sacramento, and regularly won prizes for all of his wines. A reporter writing for the *Sacramento Daily Union* in 1860 stated that Vallejo and Haraszthy exhibited their wines at the Sonoma County Fair, and that both were of "superior quality—the best indeed that I have tasted in the State."

These two pioneers were the most well-known local winemakers, but another winery had been founded even as Haraszthy was working on his plans for Buena Vista. In 1858 German immigrant Jacob Gundlach bought 400 acres south of Buena Vista and named the area Rhinefarm. The following year he and partners Emil Dresel, Charles C. Kuchel, and John Lutgens planted their first vines. Their premier vintage came out in 1861, and seven years later fellow German Charles Bundschu joined the firm, called J. Gundlach & Co. The families who ran Rhinefarm intermarried over the years, and sometime after 1894 the business was renamed Gundlach-Bundschu Wine Company.

By the mid-1870s nearly all the land west and southwest of the Plaza was planted in vineyards. Winemaking was proving to be lucrative, and many of the vintners had their wineries in town, occasionally right on the Plaza.

Sometime during this decade a collection of grape growers and winemakers formed the Sonoma Vinicultural Club. Their interest wasn't solely in agriculture and the chemistry of wine production. These were businessmen, and they met regularly to taste local and even foreign vintages and to discuss the best ways to get their grapes and wines to San Francisco and to fairs across the country. In 1875 the group met to talk about getting Sonoma wines to the US centennial celebrations to be held in Philadelphia the following year (they were not successful).

Many of the men who were part of the Vinicultural Club show up throughout the rest of the nineteenth century in newspaper and magazine articles about winemaking or grape growing. The Poppe family, originally from Germany, was known in Sonoma and nearby Glen Ellen for their grocery business, for breeding imported carp, and for making fine wines. By 1889 J. E. Poppe had a cellar full of Riesling, Traminer, and Sémillon.

By 1888 there were 136 winemakers or grape growers in Sonoma, of which 18 were women. These included the usual suspects: Agoston Haraszthy's daughter-in-law Natalia Vallejo Haraszthy, General Vallejo, the Poppes, Jacob Gundlach, and a few names that would soon adorn street signs throughout the Sonoma Valley: C. C. Carriger, O. W. Craig, and G. Chauvet.

As the nineteenth century came to a close, a new tradition took shape in Sonoma. Charles Bundschu started a wine and literary society called the Bacchus Club. In 1896 the club presented a play in Pansy Valley, near Rhinefarm, called *The Vintage Festival* or *The Bacchus Festival*. It was written by Ben Weed, Bundschu's brother-in-law and the principal of the high school. The drama, set in ancient Greece, was the story of a goatherd and the daughter of a vineyardist, who could marry only if there was a good grape crop.

Sonoma resident Harold van Coops remembered attending the play as a child. Families rode to Pansy Valley in wagons and carts or on horseback, and sat around in groups eating picnic lunches while fiddlers and other strolling musicians entertained them. At dusk, kerosene lanterns were lit and the play commenced, the highlight of which was a bright red flare announcing the coming of the god Jupiter. When the performance ended to enthusiastic applause, everyone then headed home, their paths lit by moonlight.

The Vintage Festival performance was an annual event for only a few years. In 1900 Ben Weed wasn't able to book Pansy Valley, and the play was never performed again. The concept of a harvest celebration languished, waiting for another generation to bring it back, in a new and improved form.

By the 1890s Sonoma was lucky to have something to celebrate at all. For two decades a monster had been stalking the vineyards of the Valley of the Moon. Its name was *Phylloxera vastatrix,* more commonly called the root louse.

These simple nouns—*Phylloxera vastatrix* and *root louse*—belie the horror that this insect inflicted once it took hold among the roots of grapevines. The word *Vastatrix* comes from the Latin for *destroyer,* and it was more than apt. Not only did it ravage California's vineyards, but it threatened entire winemaking regions in western Europe, especially France.

Phylloxera is native to the United States, and over the centuries indigenous grape varieties developed a resistance to its effects. In the 1850s and 1860s, grapevines from Europe were planted in California, and American vines were taken there for experiments in grafting. When the European varieties were planted in Sonoma and elsewhere, the louse attacked their roots with terrifying vigor, and they had no ability to fight it off. At the same time, the bug traveled to Europe on American grape stocks. When *Phylloxera* arrived in France, Spain, and elsewhere, it quickly went to work in local vineyards.

The louse feeds on a grapevine's roots, and because everything is happening underground, the damage isn't immediately noticeable. But soon the vines become stunted, they produce less fruit, they are more susceptible to other diseases, and eventually they die. The bug was first discovered and identified in 1873, in vineyards in Sonoma, and by 1880 at least six hundred acres had been destroyed in the valley alone. The crisis prompted the formation of the Board of State Viticultural Commissioners in that year, and its first order of business was to solve the *Phylloxera* problem.

Two years earlier, however, the winemakers of Sonoma had invited Professor Eugene Hilgard, from the University of California at Berkeley, to come and speak to them about the root louse and what to do about it. He mentioned the "melancholy piles of costly fire-wood seen about the wineries, and even in the public square," and then revealed the latest thinking about fighting *Phylloxera*.

By this time, most scientists agreed that the only way to stop the devastation was to tear out whole vineyards, replant them with resistant American grapes, and then graft the wine variety onto this rootstock. Unfortunately, not everyone had such faith in science, and for years some vineyardists turned to crackpot remedies for stopping the insect. These mostly involved applying strange substances to the soil or the vines: sulfuric acid, wood ashes, sealing wax, decoction of poppies, horse dung, olive oil, and Peruvian guano, to name a few. None proved equal to the problem.

Slowly, American grape growers came around to the solutions offered by Hilgard and others. Advertisements in farming magazines with titles such as "Resistant Vines the Only Safety" and the health of newly planted vineyards convinced the rest of the skeptics. Enthusiastic articles about California's grape crop showed up in western newspapers and magazines by the late 1880s and into 1890. Winemakers could brag about their vintages again, and advertisements featuring the Sonoma name began to appear outside of California. F. Andriessen, of Allegheny City, Pennsylvania, placed an ad in the *Pittsburgh Dispatch* in March 1889, announcing that he was selling Sonoma dry port, dry sherry, muscatel, brandies, and Angelica. There was even a Sonoma California Wine Company in Washington, DC, which advertised the "Purest and Best California Wines" during the holiday season of 1890.

In the last quarter of the nineteenth century, US and European cities held fairs and expositions to showcase their products and know-how. As the damage from *Phylloxera* slowly abated, Sonoma sent exhibits of its grapes and wines to many of these venues. In 1885 Sonoma County displayed its agricultural products at the exposition in Louisville, Kentucky, and a tower of wine was a striking feature of the display. In 1889 an exhibit called "California on Wheels" was shipped on a train to an exhibition in Lansing, Michigan, carrying several cases of Sonoma wine. Local vintners sent wine that same year to the Paris Exposition, and many of the wines won silver and bronze medals at the judging.

California also offered plenty of opportunities for winemakers to display their products closer to home. The Mechanics' Institute in San Francisco held annual fairs beginning in 1874, and Sonoma County usually had a presence there. In 1886 patrons interested in California wines were "invited to sample the Sonoma county wine exhibit," though it isn't clear whether they actually drank the wines. In 1887 Napa won first prize for the best display and quality of wine, but Sonoma came from behind to beat the rival valley the following year.

At the 1894 Midwinter Exposition in San Francisco's Golden Gate Park, California winemakers created an exhibit featuring plaster statues of Bacchus surrounded by quotes about wine in a variety of languages. Fifty-two winemakers and merchants displayed their wares, and visitors could taste some of the wines this time. Not to be outdone, the northern Sonoma County town of Cloverdale held a Citrus Fair in 1897, to show the world that there was more to county agriculture than grapes. However, a writer for the *San Francisco Call* did bring up the subject. "Everybody knows that Sonoma County wine, in the battalions of bottles that are stood up like so many soldiers all over the United States, ranks as a commander-in-chief."

By 1900 Sonoma's winemakers could breathe a sigh of relief, as the *Phylloxera* years seemed to be over. They looked ahead to a new century of expansion, experimentation, profitability, and pride. The optimism shown by valley vineyardists gave new residents the confidence to start wineries of their own. Others who had given up because of *Phylloxera* saw their properties passing into new hands.

George Hearst, the mining millionaire, father of newspaper publisher William Randolph Hearst, bought Madrone Vineyards in the nearby hamlet of Glen Ellen in 1885. It had been established as a winery as far back as 1863, and belonged to a local winemaker named Eli T. Sheppard. When Madrone was devastated by the root louse, Hearst replanted the entire vineyard with resistant stocks. After his death, his widow, Phoebe, sold the business to the California Wine Association.

Samuele Sebastiani, a native of Italy, made his way to Sonoma in 1895. In 1904 he purchased a large building and sixty acres of grapes from an uncle and started up a commercial winery just a few blocks from the Plaza.

Life wasn't completely rosy, however. When the massive earthquake of April 18, 1906, tore through San Francisco, Sonoma was also in its path, and local winemakers suffered varying degrees of damage. Buena Vista's cellars cracked and its tunnels collapsed, all beyond repair. Gundlach-Bundschu had extensive winemaking operations and family homes in San Francisco. They lost more than three million gallons of wine, in addition to three homes, and the firm reinvented itself as a smaller, estate winery. The solid stone Madrone Winery also tumbled to pieces.

In 1915 the city of San Francisco celebrated its rebirth after the earthquake—as well as the opening of the Panama Canal—with a world's fair called the Panama-Pacific International Exposition (PPIE). Displays devoted to commerce and the arts filled the exposition palaces, and the state's winemakers decided to show visitors what California and Sonoma could do. Local wine men were on the display committees, and plans were made for an exhibit of both grapes and wines in the Palace of Agriculture, as well as a sampling room. They hoped to outshine the displays from countries such as France, Spain, and Portugal, which reportedly wanted to "stem the tide that has set in in favor of California wines." Relations seemed to be cordial, though, because an official Wine Day was observed on July 14, 1915, in honor of the visiting International Congress of Viticulture.

There was another exhibit at the exposition that should have given the winemakers pause. It was created by the Anti-Saloon League, an organization devoted to trumpeting the evils of alcohol, and it was a popular stop for many visiting the fair. By 1920, when histories of the PPIE were being published, the viticulture exhibit was rarely mentioned, despite its gold medals and highly praised displays. The reason for this omission was a disaster worse than any earthquake.

Prohibition.

CRUSADES AGAINST ALCOHOL were not new in America. The temperance movement can be traced back to the beginning of the republic, and advocates used both religion and health as reasons for abstaining from liquor, or at least drinking in moderation. The first prohibition laws were enacted in the 1840s, but the movement took on more followers later in the nineteenth century, even in California. The state's Prohibition Party held its 1888 convention in San Francisco, and its platform included the statement "We denounce wine as the prostitution of the grape industry." The party had quite a few representatives from Sonoma County.

As the anti-liquor lobby gained traction, winemakers wrote and spoke about the health benefits of wine, a position held by some temperance advocates. They hoped that wine would be exempted from the ban that they knew was coming. But when the Volstead Act went into effect in 1920, wine was on the prohibited list. Viniculturists read the act carefully, looking for ways they could stay in business.

A few licenses for the production of sacramental and medicinal wine were available, and these were snatched up quickly. Samuele Sebastiani was lucky enough to acquire one of the coveted documents. Those less fortunate grew grapes for juice and raisins, and for a while the demand for both gave the locals hope, but overproduction collapsed this market by the mid-1920s.

Wine could be made at home, however, and families were allowed to make 200 gallons a year for their personal consumption. Prohibition's goal was to stop the traffic in alcohol, so home operations were not closely monitored. This led to a surge of personal winemaking that continued into the war years.

But the effect of Prohibition on wineries was devastating. In 1919 American wineries produced 55 million gallons of wine. By 1925 that number had declined to only 3,638,000. In the Sonoma Valley, many businesses failed, and others barely held on. When repeal finally came in 1933, the damage could be seen all over town: closed wineries, abandoned buildings full of discarded machinery and rotting barrels, and shabby, neglected vineyards. Even those firms that were able to get back on their feet had trouble finding experienced workers, as many had fled the valley during the dry years. But Sonoma's most profitable industry slowly began to revive, and winemakers worked hard to put Sonoma wines back on America's table.

In 1936 the business and professional men of San Francisco were treated to a wine tasting at the Palace Hotel, and many Sonoma vintages were on offer. When the Golden Gate International Exposition was held on Treasure Island in San Francisco Bay in 1939, Sonoma's winemakers joined other California vintners in creating a display in the food and beverage pavilion. "The Temple of Bacchus" exhibit demonstrated every aspect of the winemaking process, from grape crush to glass. And in possibly the first reference to wine and food pairing, the display's stated purpose was to educate the public about wine use as "a temperate table beverage and an accompaniment of food."

In March 1941, Sonoma's winemakers attended a meeting in Santa Rosa to hear experts from the marketing firm of J. Walter Thompson talk about ways in which advertising could increase sales. They were no doubt dazzled by the other speaker of the evening: Princess Alexandra Kropotkin, a columnist for *Liberty* magazine, descendant of Russian royalty, and the daughter of anarchist Peter Kropotkin. She regularly praised California wine in her columns and suggested its use in her recipes aimed at American hostesses.

December 1941 brought the United States into World War II, and Sonoma's vintners reaped unexpected benefits. Alcohol was an important raw material for the war effort. The tartaric acid produced as a result of winemaking was a vital component for the production of rayon, used for tents and parachutes. Increased production of wine meant that other by-products could be used for every aspect of wartime life. Grape pomace (the skins and seeds left over after pressing) was used for medicine, paints and cattle feed, for example.

The war years also saw the establishment of many new wineries. The forgotten Madrone vineyards were purchased in 1941 by Enrico Parducci and Peter Domenici and renamed Val-Moon. The Miglioretti brothers of Baltimore arrived in the valley in 1944. They bought the Ranch on the Knoll, once part of the old Buena Vista Vinicultural Society property, and established Embros Winery.

Four newsreel companies also traveled to Sonoma Valley in 1944 in order to film the grape harvest. The resulting footage was shown in theaters in the United States, South America, and England, as well as at American army bases worldwide. These tributes to California wine, and its importance to the war effort, helped Sonoma viniculturists finally shake off the horror of Prohibition.

Embros Winery's
"Ranch on the Knoll,"
1940s. Used by
permission.

AFTER 1945, with the war behind them, Sonoma's winemakers decided to revive an old tradition: a vintage festival. Some had broached the subject soon after repeal of the Volstead Act in 1933, viewing it as a way to celebrate the area's revival and bring tourists into town. There was also interest in besting the competition over in the Napa Valley. St. Helena had been holding yearly festivals since before Prohibition, and when there was talk of bringing back Sonoma's old Rhinefarm celebrations, they objected to the use of the term *vintage festival,* expressing the opinion that the name belonged to them. Nothing came of these discussions until October 1947, when the Valley of the Moon Vintage Festival debuted at the Plaza. Now part harvest celebration and part historical pageant, it bore no resemblance to the Greek drama of the previous century. Its committees were filled with Sonoma's elite and Sonoma's winemakers.

Buena Vista Winery was also brought back to life after the war. In the early 1940s Frank Bartholomew, a newspaperman and later head of the United Press news service, bought up the derelict property to create a country getaway. When he and his wife learned that they now owned a historic winery, they decided to return the buildings and the vineyards to their former glory. The first vintages were released in 1947 and received both praise and prizes.

Another accomplished American found his way to Sonoma too. Ambassador to Italy James D. Zellerbach and his wife, Hana, purchased two hundred acres north of the Plaza, with the intention of creating a small but high-quality winery. They named it Hanzell—a contraction of Mrs. Zellerbach's first and last names—and planted the oldest Pinot Noir vineyard in America in a six-acre plot in 1953.

Winemakers decided to try something new in the postwar years: wine tasting. Visitors to fairs and expos had been able to sample wines for decades, but tasting at a wine cellar was a novel idea. The credit for the first winery tasting probably belongs to Beringer Brothers, in St. Helena, who opened their cellars to the public in 1934. However, Charles Krug, also of St. Helena, came up with the idea of an actual tasting room around 1949.

Sonoma's wineries were soon offering tastings as well. The Vintage Festival provided one of the best opportunities for winemakers to advertise the delights of their tasting rooms. Throughout the 1950s and into the 1960s, the pages of the *Sonoma Index-Tribune* were filled with display ads aimed at tourists. The Wine Institute, an advocacy organization founded in 1934 to promote further interest in California wine, created winery maps for all of the state's regions by 1954. A rise in the sales of table wine in that decade meant that more people were interested not only in drinking California's vintages but also in seeing where they were made. Picturesque Sonoma Valley, along with its rival Napa, was a destination for thousands of fledgling wine lovers.

They were helped along by articles in magazines and newspapers that touted the drinkability of Sonoma wines, as well as the pleasures of visiting the valley itself. Wine journalism began in the 1960s, and readers learned about the great vineyards of France, the new vineyards of Sonoma, and how to go to a wine tasting without looking like a novice. As the 1970s and 1980s approached, advertising moved from the printed page to the television screen, and wine knowledge was no longer the province of the privileged.

TODAY, SONOMA WINES, and the valley they come from, are famous all over the world. The region's popularity got a big boost in the 1970s and 1980s when dozens more wineries were founded, and new businesses regularly appear around the Plaza and in the surrounding hills. Maps of Sonoma contain a veritable alphabet soup of wineries, from Arrowood, Benziger, and Cline, to Ravenswood, Robledo, and Viansa.

There are thirteen different *appellations,* or wine-growing microclimates, in the area, which means that Sonoma is known for a variety of great wines, no matter which ones happen to be in vogue at the moment. And in keeping with a trend that started in the 1880s, women winemakers continue to contribute to the quality of Sonoma's vintages.

Rivalry with the Napa Valley has only intensified over the years. A popular saying in Sonoma, seen on many bumper stickers and license plate frames, declares, "Sonoma Means Wine. Napa Means Auto Parts." The phrase is sometimes attributed to comedian Tommy Smothers, of the Smothers Brothers, who opened his Remick Ridge Vineyards in 1977, though no one really knows who said it first. It's a pithy way of expressing how the two valleys continue to compete with each other in wine, agriculture, lifestyle, and attitude.

Sonoma is a magnet for tourists who see wine as an experience, rather than simply something to drink. Tasting rituals have changed over the decades, but the essential ceremony remains, reflecting the valley's easy mix of tradition and modernity.

Some of Sonoma's original wineries are still going strong. Buena Vista, Gundlach-Bundschu, Val-Moon (now called Valley of the Moon), Sebastiani, and Hanzell are among them. Buena Vista and Sebastiani are also California State Historic Landmarks. Others are long gone—Poppe and Embros, for example, though the family has revived the Embros business and now operates out of Mendocino County.

The Plaza features wineries along its perimeter again, as it did in the 1870s. And home winemaking, with the advent of the personal wine label, saw a resurgence in the 1990s. A collective called Sonoma Home Winemakers is made up of locals who share their passion for winemaking, and who make award-winning wines each year under names such as Mt. Pisgah Cellars and JFD Estate Vineyards.

The Valley of the Moon Vintage Festival is still held every year. Some of its activities, such as the children's parade and the Mission Pageant, are no longer part of the program, but the Blessing of the Grapes inaugurates every festival.

One event has been observed at the Vintage Festival for decades: the reenactment of the 1863 Vallejo-Haraszthy wedding. The happy couples and their families, in full nineteenth-century costume, walk joyously out of the mission to the applause of the gathered crowds. The historic significance might be lost on many visitors, but in its quaint and colorful way, this ceremony embodies the importance of wine to Sonoma's past and present.

In 1859 the *Daily Alta California* printed an article titled "Vine Culture in Sonoma Valley." In his conclusion, the writer made a prediction that, more than 150 years later, seems to have come true:

> It is to these vines that the people of Sonoma look for their future prosperity. . . . They fondly hope . . . that the neighboring towns of Petaluma and Napa, which now turn up their scornful noses when the mud-built village of Sonoma is mentioned, will then bow in reverence before the rich city and fertile valley of the vine.

Chapter Five

Mr. and Mrs. London

*C*alifornia has produced some of the world's most famous authors. A few were born in the Golden State, others chose to live and write within its borders, and some are deeply associated with the regions in which they lived and worked.

For example, the works of hard-boiled Raymond Chandler and equally tough Charles Bukowski exemplify the darker side of Los Angeles. Dashiell Hammett and Mark Twain were born in the East and Midwest, but both counted San Francisco home for a time and created memorable characters there. The Central Valley gave us John Steinbeck and William Saroyan.

And Sonoma gave us Jack London.

HE DIDN'T START OFF in the Valley of the Moon, but he was a Bay Area boy. Born in San Francisco in 1876 and given the name John, the future Jack London was the child of Flora Wellman and, most likely, itinerant astrologer William Chaney. The two were not married, and Chaney did not stick around to be a father. The high-strung Flora struggled to raise her child, but was helped by Virginia Prentiss, an ex-slave who would be London's mother figure throughout his formative years.

While her son was still an infant, Flora married John London, a Civil War veteran and widower whose two youngest children, Eliza and Ida, were still at home. He worked hard to support his family despite losing a lung to pneumonia during the war years. London gave his new stepson his own last name, and by the time he was a teenager, young John London was known as Jack.

Poverty and many relocations around the San Francisco and Oakland region meant that Jack had an uneven education, but he had the great fortune to be living in Oakland when the poet Ina Coolbrith was the librarian at the Oakland Public Library. She took an interest in the bright young boy and helped steer him to the path that would eventually lead him to literature.

When he was old enough, Jack began to contribute to the family economy. He raided the Southern Pacific Railroad's private oyster beds in the bay, then turned enforcer against the oyster pirates. When he was seventeen he shipped aboard the *Sophia Sutherland* and became a seal hunter. But once home, he was forced to take menial, hard-labor jobs, becoming, in his words, a "work beast." This existence grated on his soul, and he soon joined the famous Kelly's Army of unemployed workingmen, did some hoboing, and spent time in jail in Erie County, New York. He made it back to California in 1894, still just eighteen years old. His experiences on the road exposed him to injustices that solidified his simmering political views, and he would eventually be known around Oakland as the Boy Socialist. He finished high school and even managed a semester at the University of California, Berkeley, but classroom life didn't take.

One thing had lit a fire inside him, however: writing. At his mother's suggestion, Jack had entered a literary contest sponsored by the *San Francisco Morning Call* newspaper in 1893 for the best descriptive article by a local writer under the age of twenty-two. He wrote up the experience of piloting the *Sophia Sutherland* through a typhoon off Japan, and was stunned when he won the $25 first prize. Later, at Oakland High School, his talent was recognized and encouraged by a perceptive teacher. But further forays into the writing life were delayed by the lure of yet another adventure.

In the summer of 1897 Jack and James Shepard, the husband of his stepsister Eliza, took off for the Yukon, the region of northwest Canada that was the epicenter of a frenzied gold rush. The older Shepard couldn't complete the trip and went back home, leaving Jack to find new partners. By January 1898 Jack was broke and almost broken, suffering from scurvy and the unrelenting cold. As the spring thaw approached, he made plans to return to Oakland, arriving home in the summer to find that his stepfather had died and he was expected to help support the family once more.

Jack was ready to meet his obligations, but he swore he would never be a work beast again. He would fulfill a vow he had made to himself while enduring the Yukon winter: he would become a writer.

He began to crank out stories, poems, and essays, some based on his Yukon experiences, others the fruit of his earlier years or his boundless imagination. He collected an almost equal number of rejection slips, but at the end of 1898 the *Overland Monthly* magazine offered to publish his story "To the Man on the Trail."

Started in San Francisco in 1868, the *Overland Monthly* was originally edited by Bret Harte, and was a California-focused rival of the more established *Atlantic* magazine in the East. Its pages featured writings by Mark Twain, Ambrose Bierce, and other famous westerners. After "To the Man on the Trail" appeared in the January 1899 issue, five more London stories appeared during that year.

AS JACK LONDON the former oyster pirate was poised to become Jack London the writer, the woman who would one day be central to his life and career was finding her own way in the world.

Clara Charmian Kittredge was born in Wilmington, California, in 1871, the daughter of Wisconsin native Daisy Wiley and cavalry officer Willard "Kitt" Kittredge. The two met in southern California, to which both families had emigrated from Wisconsin. Daisy was troubled by depression after her daughter's birth and for a while little Charmian was cared for by Daisy's sisters, Ninetta and Tissie.

The Kittredge family eventually moved to the Sonoma County town of Petaluma, where they ran a hotel. In 1874 it burned down, and Daisy collapsed at the loss of their livelihood. She moved to southern California to live with family members, and died there in 1876.

Ninetta became a surrogate mother again, this time with her husband, Roscoe Eames. Charmian lived with her father for a while, but she was too much for the widower to manage. Just a toddler, Charmian was then sent to live permanently with her aunt Ninetta in Oakland.

She and Roscoe had no children, and they brought Charmian up in their image: vegetarian, socialist, and feminist, a unique combination even in Bay Area Bohemian circles. They loved their niece, but expected her to pull her own weight in life, so they taught her shorthand and typing.

These skills came in handy, as Charmian became the secretary to Susan Mills, founder of Mills College in Oakland. This work helped pay for her education, but she left school after two years. The rules of the college dorm were too restrictive for her after growing up in the freethinking Eames household.

She then worked as a secretary in a San Francisco shipping firm, and as she entered her twenties, she distinguished herself by becoming a virtuoso pianist and a fearless horseback rider. She also horrified middle-class Oaklanders by riding the hills in a split skirt and without a chaperone, and by openly embarking upon affairs with men she had no intention of marrying.

By the early 1890s Ninetta and Roscoe were editors of the *Overland Monthly,* and it was Ninetta who first read and then championed Jack London's early stories. Charmian also wrote occasional reviews and articles for the publication, and early in 1899 she ran into Jack London dur-

Charmian London demonstrating her horsemanship, 1910s. Collection of the author.

ing one of his visits to her aunt's home. They saw each other infrequently over the next few years, during which time Jack became a husband and father, marrying his former math tutor, Bess Maddern, in 1900. They had two daughters: Joan, born in 1901, and Becky, born in 1902.

Jack also went from strength to strength as a writer. Beginning with *The Call of the Wild,* he published *The People of the Abyss, Children of the Frost,* and *The Kempton-Wace Letters* during 1903 and 1904.

In the summer of 1903 Jack and his family made a visit to Wake Robin Lodge, the home and collection of rental cabins owned by Ninetta and Roscoe Eames in the hamlet of Glen Ellen, a few miles from Sonoma. It had begun life as one of General Vallejo's properties, and was then acquired by southerner Charles Stuart, whose Scottish wife was named Ellen. They named their new home Glen Ellen Ranch (it's now the Glen Oaks Ranch on Highway 12). By the 1880s trainloads of summer day-trippers were flocking to the area, and by the turn of the twentieth century, Glen Ellen was the friendly sister city to the more well-known Sonoma.

The hamlet of Glen Ellen, as it appeared when first seen by Jack London. Courtesy Sonoma Valley Historical Society. Used by permission.

Charmian also spent time with her aunt and uncle in their country place. Jack's marriage was fraying at the edges, and later that year what had been a simmering attraction between Jack and Charmian turned into a passionate affair.

After separating from Bess, Jack rented one of the cottages at Wake Robin Lodge. There, sitting at a table beside a nearby creek, he wrote one of his greatest novels, *The Sea Wolf*, with Charmian typing the manuscript. It was published in 1904, the year when Jack also spent time as a war correspondent in Korea.

During 1905 both Jack and Charmian lived at Wake Robin, and their occasional horseback forays around the valley together were reported in the *Sonoma Index-Tribune* with a remarkable lack of moral judgment. In June the paper reported the rumor that the two would soon be married. What was even more interesting to readers was the news that Jack had purchased property on the northeastern slope of Sonoma Mountain, the promontory that dominates the valley for miles around.

Earlier that year Jack and Charmian had taken one of their many horseback rides in the hills above Glen Ellen. On this day the couple came across an exquisite piece of land, filled with redwoods, silent canyons, and gentle springs. It struck Jack as the kind of place where he could find real peace after the struggles he had endured over his career and his marriage during the previous years. The 128-acre tract was for sale, and Jack snatched it up, declaring to those who asked that his intention was to build a home there.

Jack's move from urban Oakland to rural Sonoma County was also of interest to readers of the *San Francisco Call*. On June 28 the paper reported that Jack, "hatless, coatless and with a shirt-collar open displaying a broad sunburnt chest," rode over to Santa Rosa to check on the titles to his new property.

Jack's divorce from Bess was final in the autumn of 1905. On November 20 he and Charmian, who called each other "Mate-Man" and "Mate-Woman," were married in Chicago, Jack's latest stop on a socialist lecture tour. By February 1906 the *Sonoma Index-Tribune* announced that the couple was back on "their big ranch."

IN TRUTH, though they owned a "big ranch," they still lived at Wake Robin Lodge, in an annex Jack built in 1905. He continued to write, and kept to a self-imposed discipline of one thousand words per day, a rule he rarely broke even in the hard last years of his life.

It was at Wake Robin, on the morning of April 18, that Jack and Charmian were tossed awake by the tremor that nearly destroyed both San Francisco and Santa Rosa. Riding toward their ranch, they found their new barn in ruins, but once they visited both devastated cities they realized how lucky they had been. Jack, as talented a photographer as he was a writer, took photos of crippled San Francisco as he and Charmian slept in doorways before the fire drove them out of town.

Back in Glen Ellen the Londons rebuilt the barn and made long-range plans to mold the ranch into their future home. In May Jack's novel *White Fang* was serialized in *Outing Magazine.* At the same time, they moved ahead with an adventure they had conceived even before they were married: a sail around the world.

Jack was an accomplished sailor, and had handled ships and boats on every kind of waterway from the mighty Pacific to the small inlets of San Francisco Bay. Early in 1906 construction began on a forty-five-foot ketch that would take them on a seven-year circumnavigation of the globe. It was named the *Snark,* in honor of Lewis Carroll's poem, in which an "improbable crew" seeks an "inconceivable creature." They left the port of San Francisco in April 1907, with high hopes and only slightly experienced crew members.

True to himself and his craft, Jack wrote his thousand words per day on the voyage, and began the semiautobiographical novel *Martin Eden.* Over the next two years the crew of the *Snark* traveled the South Pacific, and both Jack and Charmian demonstrated the boundless curiosity and extraordinary courage that made them so perfect for each other. However, serious illness and financial troubles forced them to cut the voyage short and abandon their much-loved ketch. They arrived back in Glen Ellen in July 1909, and Jack threw himself into his next great creation: his "dream-ranch," which he also sometimes called "the Ranch of Good Intentions."

Ninetta Eames was in charge of the ranch business while Jack was on the voyage. At his request, she purchased additional acreage as it came up for sale. In December 1908 she had acquired the 127 acres known as the LaMotte Ranch. By the end of 1909, when the Londons were recovered from the trials of life on the *Snark,* Jack had acquired another 30 acres of adjacent property, giving the ranch a total of nearly 300 acres. His book *Burning Daylight,* the story of a man whose urban malaise is cured by the beauty of the Sonoma Valley, also came out later that year.

The year 1910 brought both fulfillment and tragedy. Jack began to draw up plans for a magnificent home to crown what he called his "abiding place." In the spring he bought another 700 acres, which had belonged to the Kohler and Frohling winery. But in the summer, Charmian gave birth to a baby girl, named Joy, who lived for only one day.

Then, to the Londons' great good luck, Jack's stepsister Eliza and her son, Irving, came to live on the ranch after the Shepard marriage collapsed. Jack quickly handed over the management of his ranch and the supervision of the home construction to his beloved, capable, and level-headed sister.

Trips around northern California and to New York filled 1911, a year in which Jack purchased the earthquake-crumbled Kohler and Frohling winery buildings. The property also included a small cottage, into which he and Charmian moved the following year, finally leaving Wake Robin Lodge for a place of their own. The comfortable old house soon sported separate sleeping porches for Jack and Charmian, as she suffered from almost nightly insomnia.

Jack's dream home was also beginning to take shape. Renowned San Francisco architect Albert Farr had been hired to create the blueprints, and as the home came together its four stories began to resemble one of the great lodges of the West. Made of mostly local materials, it featured volcanic rock, redwood, and tile, with a gun room, a wine cellar, numerous guest rooms, a two-story living room, a library, and a workroom for the writer.

Jack, perhaps unconsciously, echoed the guiding principles of the contemporary Arts and Crafts movement, by declaring that the construction and decoration of his house must complement each other. The redwood logs were put into place with their bark intact, and the stonework inside looked just like the stone outcroppings that surrounded the house.

One of Jack's greatest friends was the poet George Sterling, who had given him the nickname Wolf. When Sterling saw the architectural plans early in the process, he immediately christened the place "Wolf House," a fitting lair for its owner.

In September 1911 Jack was hailed as a hero for leading a squad of volunteer firefighters and stopping a forest fire that menaced Glen Ellen. His dual life as rancher and writer still fascinated his public, and in November the *San Francisco Call* profiled London's bucolic existence as part of its series "Where Some California Writers Live." Reporter Henry Meade Blande applauded London's desire to stay in California after becoming a success.

The Londons were endearing themselves to the locals as well. In September 1912 the Sonoma Valley Woman's Club planned an "art and relics" exhibition at the mission in celebration of a California festival, coinciding with Admission Day. Jack and Charmian loaned some of the artifacts they had brought back from the *Snark* voyage, described as a "large and valuable collection." A special room at the mission was set up just for their display.

But Jack was also a neighbor with strict rules about his property. In October 1912, after he lost a horse to "irresponsible" hunters, he placed a display ad in the *Sonoma Index-Tribune*. He was compelled to warn the public off the ranch, and concluded by stating that all "hunters, fishers and trespassers will be prosecuted."

In January 1913 Jack bought the final block of land to make his dream complete: the former Freund Ranch, a plot of 400 acres, giving him a total of more than 1,400 acres.

Jack threw himself into his new role as rancher, though at the beginning some locals may be forgiven for thinking he would simply be a "gentleman farmer" and leave the hard work to others. They could not have been more wrong.

As early as November 1905, just a few months after buying his first parcel of land, Jack placed a large order for California native plants and bulbs from nurseryman Carl Purdy, who had established a well-known native nursery in Ukiah in the late 1870s. The *Snark* voyage had put ranch plans and improvements on hold, though Ninetta was nominally in charge of operations. But once Jack returned from the South Pacific and regained his health, it was time to put full-time sailor behind him and turn his formidable attention to the next phase of his life.

LOOKING AROUND HIS LAND, he realized that before he could get the ranch into working order, he first had to undo the obvious damage. Previous owners of the various tracts he now owned had depleted the soil to the point of sterility. Jack called this "unintelligent farming," and in order to bring the land back to life he had to take up the mantle of "scientific farming."

The scientific farming movement began in the mid-nineteenth century, and its practitioners used new technologies to develop the land without the waste and destruction of previous generations. With science, farming would be efficient and innovative, and this idea had great appeal for Jack, who said he would use his head, his judgment, and the most up-to-date knowledge to make his ranch a success.

One of the first things he did was to re-create a farming system he had seen while working as a war correspondent in Korea. There, hillsides had been terraced to help prevent erosion, and as he looked around his overworked property, he realized that he could do the same on Sonoma Mountain. He also rotated crops and planted others that rich in nitrogen.

The spectacle of a famous writer trying his hand at the plow frequently made the Bay Area papers. In November 1912 the *Oakland Tribune* printed an article titled "Jack London Ploughing." It described his work on the ranch and the beauty of both the virgin stands of trees and the land under cultivation.

The following year the *Pacific Rural Press,* the preeminent magazine for western farmers and ranchers, published an extensive article about Jack's ranch and how he was rebuilding the soil to make it fertile again. Writing with a sense of wonder, the associate editor concluded the article by praising Jack's efforts and predicting success for his enterprise.

He was always willing to try new things, whether in writing or in ranching, and in 1911 he succumbed to the claims of enthusiastic salesmen who were promoting the Australian eucalyptus. This tree, one of the gum species, was a fast grower, thrived in stony soil, and could do everything that fast-disappearing American hardwoods could. At least that was the idea.

Intrigued, Jack planted the first 16,000 eucalyptus saplings around his property in April, and by the time he was finished he had put in 65,000 trees. But it didn't take long for the craze to become a bubble, and it soon popped, since in fact the trees were no good for firewood or furniture and their shallow root systems meant that they were easily toppled. Jack was philosophical about the loss of potential income, and told himself that someday he would have beautiful groves of trees that he could enjoy (not to mention that they would help stabilize his soil).

He also met the horticulturist Luther Burbank, whose home and experimental farm in Santa Rosa were famous the world over. The developer of the Shasta daisy, the Russet Burbank potato, and countless other innovative plants had also developed a spineless cactus, which he was promoting as the perfect food for cattle in arid regions of the United States.

Jack had seen cattle grazing on cactus while in Hawaii during the *Snark* voyage, and he was intrigued with Burbank's new variety. He ordered 130 cuttings directly from Santa Rosa, but as with the eucalyptus, the promise of the cactus was greater than the production. The plants took too long to grow, required more work than anticipated, and needed more water than originally thought. By 1916 the spineless cactus was no longer being hailed as the solution to the problem of large-scale cattle feed. Jack's own notes about his crop dwindled as it became obvious that the plants would never feed his herds.

Both Jack and Charmian loved animals of all kinds, and the ranch had everything from pampered pet dogs—such as Possum, a favorite fox terrier—to breeding cattle. In 1911 a plaintive letter from Jack to the *Pacific Rural Press* was printed in the October 14 edition, much to the delight of readers:

> A wail of woe! Where under the sun can I buy a thoroughbred Jersey cow? I have answered the advertisements in your columns, and all the offerings I get in reply to my letters are bulls, bulls, bulls. I haven't learned the art of milking a bull. What I want is a thoroughbred Jersey cow. Can you give me any clew for the obtaining of same.

Beneath the text of the letter a sympathetic editor printed, "Surely some generous reader will let go a cow at Mr. London."

Over the next few years Jack and Charmian traveled throughout California to find stock for their ranch. In February 1913 they were in Modesto on the trail of more Jerseys. And by 1916 cattle from the London ranch were winning prizes at various county fairs around the state. Their manure did not go to waste either. Manure from the cow barn was deposited into a cement collection tank, then drained into pipes and onto wagons. The liquid fertilizer was then sprayed on the crops.

The Londons added other animal species to the inventory as well. In 1914 a herd of goats had been pressed into service to clear some hillsides of weed growth after a year of heavy rains.

Pigs were one of London's passions, and he regularly purchased pigs and sold those raised on the ranch, especially the Duroc and Chester Boar breeds. In 1915 he astonished everyone by building what his neighbors dubbed the "Pig Palace." The *Pacific Rural Press* called it a "pig hostelry," but London called it simply his "piggery." A circular, two-story concrete feed house sat in the center of a ring of individual pens, also made of concrete. Each pig family had a set of apartments, complete with courtyard, outside run, and water troughs. A valve on the feed silo spread food to each set of pens, and another sent water into the troughs.

Jack London's "Pig Palace." Courtesy Sonoma Valley Historical Society. Used by permission.

A visitor to the ranch said that the Pig Palace was a model of "solidity, service and sanitation." Jack was very proud of his piggery, informing all who came by that he had designed the entire setup himself. The concrete palace made it easy for just one man to care for as many as two hundred pigs. His method also meant the pigs lived in more sanitary conditions, keeping diseases such as cholera at bay.

He also built the first concrete block silos in California, filling them with animal feed from nearby ranches as well as his own.

All farm animals came under his purview, but it was horses that he and Charmian treasured most. Jack had not grown up on horses as Charmian had, and he could never match her skill in the saddle. He did better with reins in his hand driving a team than actually sitting on a horse, but he loved the animals just the same. With practice he became proficient as a rider and also found pleasure in it, as he and Charmian spent many hours riding the trails around their home.

Jack preferred horses to machinery when it came to ranch work. The best draft horses were Shires, and in 1913 he purchased a one-ton Shire named Neuadd Hillside, from the Wheatley farm in Napa, which had won prizes in England and California, including at the state fair. But he was more than just a puller of plows to Jack and Charmian. It was easy for them to fall in love with horses, and Neuadd Hillside, whom they nicknamed the Great Gentleman, was one of the loves of their life.

Jack London with Neuadd Hillside. Courtesy Sonoma Valley Historical Society. Used by permission.

CHARMIAN HAD NOT BEEN IDLE while Jack was creating his dream ranch. A woman of great discipline, and a natural athlete, she rode her horse, practiced the piano, read widely, did daily calisthenics, and ran the household. She also continued to serve as Jack's typist as he filled their home with the manuscripts that were published as books or serialized in magazines. *Martin Eden, The Cruise of the Snark, South Sea Tales, Smoke Bellew,* and *John Barleycorn* were all written even as Jack bought cows and swine, supervised the construction of pig pens, and read voraciously about irrigation, the classification of livestock, and butter making.

In 1913 he published the novel *The Valley of the Moon,* a story about, and a love letter to, his new home. Main characters Billy and Saxon are a thinly disguised Jack and Charmian, and the reward for their struggles as urban work beasts is the discovery, at the end of the novel, of the Sonoma Valley, their new home.

Even before the manuscript was serialized and then published in book form, Jack was lauded as a Sonoma booster. Charles Spindler, who penned a regular column about local happenings for the *Sonoma Index-Tribune,* wrote in 1912 that Jack's books and writings about the Sonoma Valley left a deep impression in the minds of readers. Echoing the hopes of no doubt many other Sonomans, Spindler concluded, "I hope he will continue to use his pen for the benefit of our valley, so that our children will erect a monument to his memory."

Jack's movements around town were avidly reported in the paper, as he came into Sonoma proper to do errands, visit, and drink with the locals. In 1911 he rode into town to cast his vote on a simmering social issue: women's suffrage. Each state could decide whether women would be allowed to vote, and Jack checked the "Yes" box on his ballot. This was a surprise to Charmian, but as he related in his "drinking memoir" *John Barleycorn,* he decided that if women had the vote, they would someday enact a prohibition against liquor, and then he would be able to stop.

Locals selling real estate invoked Jack's popularity and his words when placing ads in newspapers all over the Bay Area. A man selling his ranch in the northern Sonoma County community of Healdsburg stated that his property was in the part of the state that Jack London termed "the Paradise of the Earth."

Jack's books and his expansive personality brought many visitors to the ranch and to Sonoma. Childhood friends and early-twentieth-century celebrities alike found their way to Jack's door.

Famed anarchist Emma Goldman and her lover, Ben Reitman, spent a few days with the Londons in April and early May of 1910. Jack invited the notorious woman for a visit even though the two had never met. After her time at the ranch she wrote one of the most quoted descriptions of Jack London, the Boy Socialist: "Here was youth, exuberance, throbbing life."

Poet and best friend George Sterling and his wife, Carrie, were frequent guests. Another literary visitor was San Francisco writer J. Allan Dunn, who had met Jack when he wrote an article about the author for *Sunset* magazine. He came by the ranch often in 1913, but eventually wore out his welcome. He turned out to be a kleptomaniac who regularly pinched items from the homes in which he was a guest. During one stay at the ranch he stole a few sets of Jack's silk pajamas.

THE LAST YEARS OF JACK LONDON'S LIFE were not easy. In 1912 Charmian miscarried another child, and the surgery needed to save her life meant they could never conceive again. This was devastating enough, but it can be argued that the seeds of Jack's too early death were sown in the summer of 1913.

Wolf House was nearly complete, and Jack and Charmian were packing and making ready to move into their new home. But on August 22, during a searingly hot night, the interior of the house caught fire, burning with such intensity that the entire building was destroyed before anything could be done to stop it.

Over the years, explanations of how the fire started have ranged from arson to accident. The most recent, and the most logical, research points to a pile of linseed-oil rags left behind by some workmen. In the summer heat they spontaneously combusted and quickly ignited the wooden floor and paneling. When the fire was finally out, all that was left was the stonework shell.

The Londons were not the only ones who grieved the loss of their dream house. The stonemason and his workers wandered the property in shock. Eliza Shepard, who had supervised every aspect of the construction, was, in Charmian's words, "scarred to the soul."

But true to both of their natures, Jack and Charmian pulled themselves together to get on with their lives. Jack built a light-filled annex onto the cottage where they were living, using it as his writing room. And despite recurring illnesses resulting from advancing kidney failure, he continued to work and travel.

In 1914 he published *The Mutiny of the Elsinore,* and went to Mexico to cover the civil war, though once in the country he found little war and much suffering to write about instead. In September both he and Charmian needed a change of scene, and they sailed the Sacramento Delta on Jack's boat the *Roamer* for a few weeks, and then spent some time in the Sierras near Lake Tahoe over the winter.

But once back at home, they found that the cold of the Sonoma Valley was hard on London's growing rheumatism, and they decided to leave town again. After a stopover in San Francisco to see the opening of the Panama-Pacific International Exposition, Jack and Charmian left for Hawaii in February 1915, where they had made happy memories during their time on the *Snark.* They returned to Sonoma in July, but went back to Hawaii again in December 1915, hoping to regain the health and equilibrium of their previous visit.

In July 1916 they were back at the ranch, and Jack proceeded to publish *The Star Rover* and *Little Lady of the Big House,* as well as a number of shorter works. He had begun to feel politically disillusioned and earlier in the year had resigned from the Socialist Party. His days were almost always filled with illness, and as autumn approached he tried to ignore his physical failings by throwing himself into ranch life again.

But he had to face another cruel blow. Neuadd Hillside, the Great Gentleman, suffered a rupture and died suddenly at the end of October. Jack was not ashamed to shed tears, but Charmian worried about the unaccustomed listlessness that he displayed over the following days and weeks.

He rallied enough in mid-November to pose for a moving picture crew, which shot him driving a team of draft horses and checking the hoof of another as Charmian sat in the saddle. Standing in the Pig Palace, he smiled and laughed as he cradled an armful of piglets.

On November 21 Jack suffered a bout of vomiting, and his dinner did not agree with him. He retired to his sleeping porch, and when she went to bed herself, Charmian could see him there, dozing over a book.

The next morning she was yanked into consciousness by Eliza and one of the cottage's servants: Jack would not wake up. A doctor was sent for, and managed to get Jack on his feet to walk about the room, but it was no use. Charmian's Mate-Man died just before 8:00 PM on November 22.

He was forty years old.

Given how hard Jack drove himself, and the multiple illnesses that plagued him at the end of his life, various fans and investigators have labeled his death everything from suicide to accidental morphine overdose. But the most likely cause was kidney failure complicated by morphine, which he had been prescribed for pain.

A casket was soon brought to the ranch, Jack was laid out in a suit, and he was transported by his workers to the train station for the trip to Oakland, accompanied by Eliza. His body was cremated and his ashes placed in a copper urn. The funeral service was held in Oakland, attended by Jack's former wife, daughters, stepsister, and friends. George Sterling read a poem he composed for his Wolf, whom he described as having an unfearing heart and an unresting mind.

Charmian had stayed in Sonoma, and on November 26 Sterling brought Jack's ashes back to the ranch. Jack had once told her that he wouldn't mind being buried on the small knoll about a half mile from

Jack London's grave. Collection of the author.

the cottage, near the graves of two pioneer children, David and Lillie Greenlaw. It was there that she buried the urn and had it cemented in place. A mossy lava boulder, meant for Wolf House but rejected by the architect, was then rolled over it.

The *Day Book,* a Chicago newspaper founded in 1911 as an "advertisement free" sheet, and unusually sympathetic to the working class, had covered Jack's life and literature for years. Its edition of November 23 printed what is probably the best headline about the writer's death: "Jack London Has Taken his Last Cruise on the Snark."

ELIZA AND CHARMIAN worked together over the next few decades to keep Jack's ranch in operation and his books in front of readers. Eliza traveled throughout the Bay Area to continue her role as stock purchaser, and her pigs and cattle won awards at fairs year after year. She managed the workers, handled accounts and legal issues, and worked as hard on the ranch as any man.

She also hired women to help with farm chores. In 1918 she had seven young women on hand to pick prunes and fill silos. Dubbed "farmerettes" by the *Sonoma Index-Tribune,* Eliza's female farm hands were described as "just all right." The next year, when many of the male farm hands enlisted to fight in World War I, Charmian donned jodhpurs to help bale hay.

Eliza raised her son, Irving, on the ranch, eventually moving into the home that Jack built for the two of them. In May 1918 Charmian hosted an engagement party for Irving and his future bride at the ranch, decorating the table in red, white, and blue, in honor of those who were at war.

Eliza was an active member of a number of patriotic organizations, both during and after the war. As tough as her beloved little brother, she had no trouble crowing about her accomplishments to the locals, and because she was so highly respected, her triumphs were their triumphs as well.

She and Charmian hosted myriad visitors to the ranch over the next few years, as a way to enjoy themselves and to keep the ranch in the public eye. In 1917 a Hawaiian couple visiting the States to buy horses for their property in the islands spent time on the ranch to look at Eliza's stock before heading off to Kentucky. The following month the California Writers' Club made what they called a "pilgrimage" to the ranch, where Charmian hosted them in her home for coffee after the group ate lunch among the trees.

War heroes were also welcomed, as were the members of the Sierra Club, who spent time hiking around local points of interest. And in the 1920s, troops of Camp Fire Girls got personalized tours of the ranch from Eliza herself.

The influx of visitors often brought problems, however. Pilgrims who wanted to be close to where Jack had written his books tended to just show up on the property. So many of them were wandering around that Charmian was forced to place a notice in the paper stating that anyone wanting to visit had to phone for permission first.

Thievery was also a problem. A bell that Jack had brought back from Korea and hung from a tree near the cottage disappeared in 1927. Three years later, Walter and Celeste Murphy, owners of the *Sonoma Index-Tribune* and close friends of Charmian's, bought the bell at a market in Mexico City. They had no idea it had come from the ranch until Charmian saw it hanging from the chandelier in their home one evening when she went to dinner.

By the 1930s, the high cost of managing the ranch caused Charmian and Eliza to make a drastic decision: they opened the ranch to guests. As with so many other western working ranches, taking in paying guests was often the only way to make ends meet. From 1935 until after World War II, the "Jack London Ranch" hosted visitors from around the world, offering horseback riding, hiking, badminton, swimming, tennis, and informal California living in rooms that had once heard the voice of the famous author.

Charmian London, 1923. Collection of the author.

Over the years, Charmian endeared herself to Sonomans by staying on the ranch and devoting time and travel to promoting Jack and his books. Even as she aged, she continued to ride her horse around the hills, stopping occasionally to chat with the locals she encountered. She was always a modern woman, and when she bobbed her hair the event made news across California and many local women followed her example.

With Eliza in charge of the ranch, Charmian was able to travel again, and both New York and Europe beckoned. She also put her own hand to the typewriter, writing stories of Hawaii as well as a biography of Jack. Many of Jack's books and stories were made into movies from the 1920s to the 1940s, but Charmian had little artistic control over the scripts and had to occasionally take producers to court over copyright infringement.

In 1934 Charmian moved into the new house she had built on the property, which was meant to be a memorial to Jack. She dubbed it "the House of Happy Walls," as it was filled with the artifacts of their life together. Five years later, Eliza passed away at the age of seventy-one, leaving Charmian bereft at the loss of the woman who had become like a sister to her.

Charmian lived in the house until she was well into her seventies, when age, a fall, and a series of strokes forced her to move back to the cottage, where she could be more easily cared for. It was only in these last years that she gave up her signature red hair and let the color go naturally gray.

On January 12, 1955, Charmian took a short walk around the property with Eliza's grandson Milo Shepard, as interested as ever, and as active as she could be. Sometime during the night, she passed away in her sleep, at the age of eighty-three. Her body was cremated and her ashes placed under the lava rock by the pioneer cemetery, next to her Mate-Man.

The great wish of her widowhood was that Jack's memory would live on. Today, the Jack London State Historic Park fulfills that wish as it hosts new generations of readers and throngs of visitors to the museum that Charmian created in her House of Happy Walls.

Chapter Six

The Tourist Trade

*V*isitors have made their way to the Sonoma Valley for more than 150 years, intrigued by its natural beauty, its quaint old adobes, and the legendary hospitality of General Vallejo.

Early in its history, men (usually) made the arduous trip from San Francisco or other parts of the state to take in the sights, go hunting and fishing, or enjoy some of the occasional festivals held on the Plaza. Many of them published their travels in Bay Area newspapers, some of which sound as though they were written by real estate speculators, such as this one from 1848: "In every direction, can be traced the almost magic progression of enterprise in its might. New lands under cultivation, and continuous building on street and square. Only a few miles distant from Sonoma, a serviceable saw-mill is in constant operation." A different writer was even more positive about Sonoma's future, in an article published just two months later: "A more healthy site for a city cannot be found in any territory belonging to the United States."

Others came to Sonoma for the kind of outdoor fun that could only be had outside of San Francisco. A writer known only as PACIFIC published an article about a Sonoma Valley excursion he took in company with a number of friends, also in 1848: "Fishing, talking, eating, drinking, dancing, and games, varied the amusements of the day, with an interlude of killing two skunks, which very audaciously came trotting over the prairie with their striped bushy tails curled over their backs, just where the ladies were sitting; and it required the greatest exertions of the cavalleros to stop these feline perfumers."

Not everyone had a good time in town, however. A few used Sonoma's popularity to further some less-than-honorable ends. In July 1855 a local man who worked in the Pacific Express office wrote to a friend in Massachusetts about life in town. Most business was conducted in the evenings and on Sundays, he said, and murders were very common. Prudent men went out in the evening armed with either a pistol or a knife. However, he did enjoy the recent Independence Day celebrations, saying that the day passed off beautifully, and only two men were shot.

In 1875 the local stagecoach was held up by three masked highwaymen who took off with $6,000 from the Wells Fargo treasure box. The robbers left the letters and papers in the box, gave it back to the stage driver, and sent him on his way.

Getting to Sonoma in the early years was not easy. Originally chosen because of its proximity to both potential mission converts and a good water supply, it was isolated for a reason. As gold seekers passed by and through town on their way to the American River, however, word spread about the fine accommodations and the excellent stores and restaurants. If you were already in the area north of San Francisco, it was a relatively easy ride over the hills to the valley. However, if you were in San Francisco or points south, the fastest way to get to Sonoma was by boat, across the bays and inlets that flowed into and out of San Francisco Bay.

One of the first men to see the potential for water transportation was William Leidesdorff, a native of the Virgin Islands. His father was a Danish planter and his mother a local woman of African and Spanish descent. In 1841, at the age of thirty-one, Leidesdorff arrived in San Francisco, by this time the captain of an American schooner and a wealthy cotton broker. He decided to stay, and became even wealthier by acquiring real estate and building hotels and warehouses. He also served as city treasurer and school board chair. In 1847 he realized the commercial potential of steamship service on San Francisco Bay, and in August his first ship began to take travelers to points around the bay, including the landing in San Pablo Bay near Sonoma Creek.

In December 1847 some prominent local citizens took a ride on the steamer as it puffed up the creek while they enjoyed dinner, cigars, and toasts to Leidesdorff. General Vallejo, his secretary, Victor Prudon, and alcalde Lilburn Boggs were part of the group. They had a lot to celebrate: the steamships would soon bring even more people to Sonoma, and connect it more closely to San Francisco, the commercial hub of the Pacific.

By 1850 visitors who took the steamer from San Francisco got off at a landing in San Pablo Bay near today's small community of Schellville. This spot had been used since mission times as the closest landfall to Sonoma, and was now given the grand name of Embarcadero, or "place of embarkation." It was about three miles from the Plaza, and its primitive but serviceable buildings—three houses and a collection of fishing boats—were collectively known as the town of San Luis or St. Louis. The steamer *Georgiana* ran three days a week between San Francisco and Sonoma. Once passengers disembarked, stages took them into town, though some decided to save a little money and walked instead. Getting to the valley from the east was a bit easier: a stage line ran three days a week between Napa, Benicia, and Sonoma.

In the early 1850s Sonoma's Embarcadero and nearby San Luis were well known and considered very prime real estate. In August 1853 Robert Graham, a farmer planning to leave California, offered up his property "opposite the town of St. Louis" for sale. Described as a splendid investment, his farm had 475 acres of fenced land, livestock, two houses, and a cargo ship capable of carrying 600 tons of goods. He also made sure to advise potential purchasers that the area was not subject to flooding.

By the early 1860s the *Peytona* took over as the regular Sonoma steamer, and it proved to be invaluable for both passengers and freight. Being able to import and export goods via the steamer was vitally important to Sonoma's merchants and to those throughout California who relied on the produce, hides, and other commodities that came from the valley. It even provided moments of excitement: in March 1861 passengers on the steamer headed to Sonoma saw a whale at the outer entrance to San Francisco Bay, and were thrilled when he spouted a few times before disappearing under the surface. Other steamers, such as the *Princess,* the *Alice,* and the *James M. Donahue,* took over as entrepreneurs in Sonoma began to manage steamer and stage service. The summer of 1888 was particularly abundant in fruit shipments from the valley to San Francisco, and the Embarcadero was busier than ever. As the *Sonoma Index* reported, "The Embarcadero people are among the most pleasant and sociable in our valley and we know whereof we speak when we say they never get the blues down that way. One always finds them the same—genial, entertaining and happy."

Steamer service was efficient and speedy, but the same could not be said of the stage service from the landing into Sonoma proper. No matter how well maintained the road, it was still a lumpy, bumpy ride into town. However, as the Civil War was coming to a close, some local men and outside investors began to think about building a railroad to link Sonoma to the steamer and to other points around the northern bay region. The advantages to business and agriculture were obvious to everyone, and the topic was discussed in newspapers and magazines all over the state. Enthusiastic meetings were also held in Sonoma, often accompanied by band music and artillery volleys.

In 1875 plans for a local railroad materialized when a group of men from Sonoma and San Francisco filed articles of incorporation for a new company. Its goal was to build a single-track railroad from the Embarcadero into town. The track and the cars themselves would be made in San Francisco. The survey of the area took place in February. The idea for the new railway was the brainchild of a San Francisco promoter named Joseph S. Kohn, and the actual name of the railroad was the Crew Prismoidal One-Rail System. The "prismoidal" part of the name referred to the unique triangular beam that formed the track, which was fifteen inches high. An iron rail was placed on top of the beam, and the train ran on this rail. Today, we would call it a monorail, but in 1875 it was a revolutionary, if wordy way to look at mass transit.

Kohn had seen this type of railroad demonstrated at industrial expositions in the Midwest and tried to sell it to the city of San Francisco, but couldn't drum up any interest. He then turned his attention to the north and convinced prominent citizens in Sonoma that his system would be perfect for moving people and produce from the Embarcadero landing into town. He envisioned his new railway as an alternative to traditional narrow-gauge railroads, in both function and cost.

In June 1876 grading for the new tracks began, starting at the bay landing on Sonoma Creek now called Wingo, but at the time named Norfolk. Construction began in August, and that same month a working prismoidal railroad was demonstrated at the Mechanics' Fair in San Francisco. By November three and a half miles of track had been completed.

To inaugurate and spark publicity for the new system, a collection of influential San Franciscans was invited to ride the prismoidal railroad on November 24, 1876. They took the steamer to Norfolk, and after disembarking on the dock they were invited to inspect the train. They climbed aboard with an understandable amount of trepidation. Everyone had ridden standard-gauge railroads before, but everything about this new railway was new, especially its rather top-heavy construction. As a reporter for the *San Francisco Examiner* put it, "A certain assurance that the whole thing would topple over at the first movement was the general belief of the uninitiated." That didn't happen, and all the passengers were delighted with the experience.

Unfortunately, the prismoidal system had one flaw: the special prism or triangular shape could not be built on a grade, so the track made it only as far as present-day Schellville. There was nothing Kohn could do, so he changed tactics and tried to convince transit officials in San Francisco that a prismoidal railway would be perfect for Market Street, but he was turned down. And with the failure of construction in the Sonoma Valley, Kohn gave up on the prismoidal system.

He was still interested in running a train into Sonoma, however. In July 1878 he formed the Sonoma Valley Railroad and obtained a right-of-way to construct a standard-gauge railroad from Schellville to the Plaza. Later that year everything came to a halt when Kohn ran out of money, but the following year the railroad caught the interest of Peter Donahue, co-founder (with his two brothers) of San Francisco's Union Iron Works and an early railroad entrepreneur. He owned the San Francisco and North Pacific Railroad (SF&NP) and was also running some of the steam ferries that carried passengers from San Francisco to the Embarcadero landing.

Donahue got Sonoma County to agree to let him build a new rail line from the Embarcadero, which would connect with Kohn's old line at Wingo, then wind its way along Eighth Street East to Spain Street and

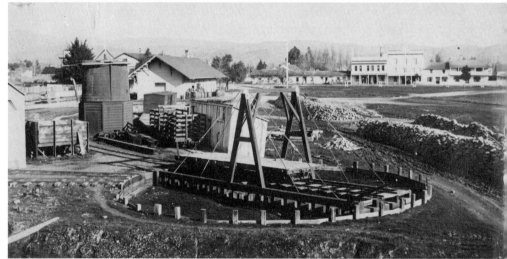

TOP: The Northwestern Pacific depot in Sonoma, ca. 1910. Courtesy Sonoma Valley Historical Society. Used by permission.

BOTTOM: The railroad yard on the Plaza before 1890. Courtesy Sonoma Valley Historical Society. Used by permission.

then west toward the center of town. A depot, car sheds, roundhouse, and other buildings were soon built on the Plaza's northern side.

Despite the value of the railroad to local business, many people in town thought that it would spoil Sonoma's unique and quiet character. There was more opposition than Donahue expected, so in order to finish the railway he set his crews to work at night. On a December morning in 1879, locals watched in awe as a large engine bearing the name *The General Vallejo* puffed along the brand-new tracks past the mission, halting noisily in front of the Plaza. Vallejo himself, his wife, daughters, and grandchildren were there to greet the train and drape it with floral tributes. Like it or not, the railroad was in town to stay. In 1880 Peter Donahue folded the Sonoma Valley Railroad into his SF&NP company, and it soon became part of everyday life in Sonoma.

Henry Weyl, however, was not happy at all. The owner of Weyl Hall on the corner of Spain Street and First Street West, he also owned the land adjacent to the plot where the depot had been built. The city had given Donahue permission to build the depot, but the tracks went right in front of Weyl's property. He sued the railroad to remove the tracks and won his case. Although the SF&NP appealed to the California Supreme Court, the appeal was denied, and the company was forced to relocate the train tracks. In 1890 the tracks were rebuilt behind Spain Street, and the depot also moved to what is today's Depot Park.

Other railways made their way into points around the Sonoma Valley in the 1880s, and by the time the depot was at its new permanent home off the Plaza, the trip from San Francisco to Sonoma was a simple and comfortable train ride. The railroads also made possible the creation of two other local small communities.

In 1879 a railroad depot was built near the property of landowner Theodore Schell and the spot christened Schellville. It was close enough to the steamer landings that it was also handy for ship travelers. A decade later, the area had hotels, stores, and a post office, but when the railroad bypassed the area and steamers no longer landed, Schellville declined. Today it is an important landmark for drivers traveling between the Sonoma and Napa valleys.

Tiny Vineburg was also a railroad stop, as its depot sat squarely on Eighth Street East, along the tracks from the old Embarcadero and along another road between Marin and Napa. It also boasted stores, a post office, a bar, a fruit packing shed, and a baseball diamond. But the demise of the railroads in the 1940s meant the end of Vineburg's prominence also.

The railroads brought more people into the Sonoma Valley to enjoy the local sights, and traffic increased as schedules expanded. At the same time, a few enterprising newcomers discovered that the valley had something else to offer the new influx of tourists, and it was right underneath their feet.

THE SONOMA VALLEY sits in the midst of a very large expanse of geothermal springs. This field ranges from Geyserville in the north to Calistoga in the east, and in the Valley of the Moon, the sites were about a mile west of the Plaza, along today's Highway 12. The natural bubbling hot mineral springs had been used for centuries by local Indians as a way to soothe the body's aches, and there may also have been rituals associated with the waters that came out of the earth. When European, Mexican, and American settlers started to flow into the area, they soon realized the medicinal and commercial value of the springs.

As early as 1848 a warm spring called Annenthal was advertised in San Francisco papers. "NO MORE RHEUMATISM!" was its motto, and a man named Andrew Hoeppener invited sufferers to visit his establishment in order to take the waters—or, as he put it, the "Warm Bath." It didn't last very long, but five years later a visitor to the valley remembered it and predicted that the springs would attract attention again. The reason was the situation of the valley itself. It was such a healthy place to live, he said, that local doctors had to take on other occupations in order to pay their bills, there being so few demands for their services.

In the 1850s Thaddeus Leavenworth, an Episcopal minister and former alcalde of San Francisco, obtained a land grant for the area called Agua Caliente—Spanish for "hot water"—in the springs area where Annenthal had once been located. He eventually held hundreds of acres in the area, but never did anything commercial with the mineral waters on his property.

The springs were used only sporadically during the years of the Civil War and Sonoma's growth as an American city, but Sonoma retained its reputation as a place where health came naturally. In July 1881, a man named George left his home in San Francisco to spend time in Sonoma, where his mother was also staying. He sent affectionate letters to a Sophie Landesberger about some unnamed ailments and how the valley was doing its job to make him feel better. On July 31 he wrote, "Well, here I am in Sonoma, the very place I have been looking for. I already feel so well that I hardly have the conscience to stay a whole week away from you." Raving about the delicious chicken and cream he was served at his boardinghouse, as well as the abundance of local fruit, George told Sophie, "If you could only be transferred from your world of drudgery and sea of dish water to this quiet land of chicken and cream with nothing to do but sleep, eat and drive with no care or thought."

By the mid-1880s the natural springs outside of town were being harnessed, formed into pools and surrounded with bathhouses by entrepreneurs who would soon strike it rich with sickly residents of California and the West. The first of these was Captain Henry Boyes. Born in England in 1844, he went into the navy and spent time in India. He retired in 1883, and as his wife was in poor health, he decided to visit the San Francisco area, hoping that the climate would be beneficial for her.

The oak arbor at the Boyes Hot Springs resort, 1913. Collection of the author.

He heard about the Sonoma Valley and met General Vallejo there, who allegedly told him about how the Indians used the mineral springs for healing. Boyes and his wife decided to settle in the valley.

Taking the general at his word, they began to dig on the property they purchased outside of town and discovered a natural hot spring. They then bought more land and began to develop the area by sinking wells and constructing a hotel, bathhouses, cottages, and campgrounds. They named their new enterprise Boyes Hot Springs and started to advertise its amenities around the Bay Area. By this time there were two trains that made their way into the valley, which meant that stays at the springs were very convenient. Visitors swam in the naturally hot water and also drank it for its mineral content (certainly not for its taste). Both were considered beneficial for all kinds of ailments.

Doctors and valley boosters published enthusiastic books and pamphlets about the springs over the next few decades. One of them was Dr. F. C. S. Sanders of Cambridge University in England. In 1916 he wrote *California as a Health Resort* and included information on Boyes Hot Springs, as well as all of the others that sprang up in the area at the end of the nineteenth century. According to Dr. Sanders, the temperature of the water at Boyes was 114 degrees and was primarily saline with a very high proportion of silica. The resort also bottled and sold its water to clients and curious tourists.

Captain Boyes was a familiar figure around the valley, always known by his military title, and his activities were usually considered news. In November 1885, for example, the *Sonoma Index-Tribune* reported on some peculiar items that he found while cleaning out one of the springs on his property. Underneath the floorboards of an old building, constructed near the waters by a previous owner, Boyes found a soup dish, a red clay pipe, a black bottle, and an eighteen-inch lock of light blond hair. A few years later, the remains of a prehistoric horse were found at another site on his property, identical to another set of fossilized remains recovered nearby. More welcome was the discovery of natural gas on Boyes's nearby farm, Agua Rica. Development of the gas deposit never went past the planning stage, however.

By the early 1900s Boyes Hot Springs was owned by R. G. Lichtenberg and Dr. E. L. Parramore. The men printed up beautiful, detailed booklets with information about the waters, swimming tanks, train service, accommodations, and recreation at their establishment. A little bit of historical exaggeration served to romance the resort's story: "Everything connected with Boyes Hot Springs is new, modern and strictly up to date, except the spring—they are the product of nature forces and the date of their original discovery is not definitely known; suffice it to say that their medicinal qualities were recognized by the old Spanish padres over one hundred years ago, and have proven a great boon to mankind ever since."

There was a new emphasis on hygiene in the early twentieth century, which Lichtenberg and Parramore made sure to address. "The tubs are cared for by careful attendants and are thoroughly cleansed and disinfected after each bath." In 1912 visitors to the bathhouse could watch a demonstration of a new "vacuum clothes washer," further evidence of the resort's commitment to fine service.

Boyes Hot Springs also catered to visitors who simply wanted a getaway from their normal routine and, perhaps, city surroundings. One booklet described the springs as the "Ideal Spot for Health and Pleasure Seekers." To meet the needs of the latter group, the resort had boats and canoes for rent, picnic grounds, fishing streams, saddle horses, and a garage for those who drove their own automobiles to the area rather than taking the train.

Boyes and its amenities were so well known that groups, as well as individuals, made their way to the valley. The Harmonie Gesang Verein, a German-American club, held its annual outing there, though the 1909 get-together was almost spoiled when an unwelcome visitor hopped off the train at Boyes Hot Springs station: former San Francisco mayor Eugene Schmitz. Three years earlier, as the dust from the 1906 earthquake and fire was still settling, Schmitz had been convicted of graft and bribery charges relating to his time in office. Although his conviction was overturned, he was persona non grata to many, including most of the members of the Verein. He was roundly snubbed, especially when he asked to address the group (although some members were pleased to be sharing a beer with such a famous person, however bad his reputation). In 1912 the Custom Cutters Association, a group of tailors and men in the clothing trade, held their annual country meeting at Boyes, where they had a dinner and a baseball game pitting the woolens men against the trimmings men.

Boyes Hot Springs also offered lots for the construction of summer homes in 1913. The development—named Sonoma Vista—was within walking distance of the resort, just across an "artistic" bridge over Sonoma Creek. Homes started at $1,500 and a mini real estate boom took place over the course of the spring. Advertisements, on-site salesmen, tours, special excursion trains, and a free lunch brought thousands of people to the area to view the lots and the existing bungalows. The homes did get built and sold, but one of the developer's plans thankfully did not make it past the drawing board: a twenty-foot-high, fourteen-foot-thick dam on Sonoma Creek, which would have created a two-mile-long lake. Had it been built, the entire area known today as the Springs would be underwater, and Sonoma itself might be only a stoplight on the way to Napa.

BOYES MAY HAVE BEEN the biggest resort in the area, but it wasn't the only one. There was plenty of hot water to go around.

By 1887 a place called Agua Caliente Warm Springs offered visitors the use of new mineral pools, and the following year M. K. Cady laid out a town site with the same name (sometimes just called Agua Caliente Springs). Two years later the spot featured a post office, a schoolhouse, the Agua Caliente Springs Hotel, a dry goods store, and a blacksmith. It was also on the railway line, making visits convenient. By the turn of the century it was a powerful rival to Boyes Hot Springs for resort business, and it placed well-written articles in San Francisco papers about its amenities: renovated hotel buildings, first-class meals, and new plunge baths. It was also, of course, "clean and neat."

One of the groups that Agua Caliente lured to its facility in the summer of 1896 was the League of the Cross, a young men's Catholic organization, which set up an outdoor camp in order to enjoy both the discipline of self-imposed military order and the proximity to the cooling waters of Sonoma Creek. It was such a hot July that the boys were barely tempted to eat, and "there was some threat of putting the butter in the guardhouse to keep it from running away." They also went to the local dances.

Advertisement for Caliente Villa, 1920s. Collection of the author.

Every resort worth visiting held entertainments for visitors, usually dances. In 1910 a woman named Margie was staying at Agua Caliente and penned postcards to her friend Viola in San Francisco. "We are up here for a week and are having a good time," she wrote on August 21. "Went down to Boyes to a dance last night. Am able to swim a little now, and am very proud of it."

Around 1910 new home lots were offered for sale in a development named Agua Caliente Park. The hotels, mineral baths, and train depot of Agua Caliente and Boyes were just one to three blocks from the tract. The property itself had a "Chalybeate" spring running through it, an iron salt considered to be a tonic for the stomach and a blood builder, according to the advertisement in the *San Francisco Call* newspaper.

Building on the success of Boyes and Agua Caliente, around 1910 a man named J. B. Morris opened a place called Home Farm just a quarter mile from Agua Caliente. A first-class table, bathing, a tennis court, and croquet were offered to visitors, with special rates for families. Within a few years Agua Caliente Park was built on the east side of what became Highway 12. The carved stone pillars that announced the fine road leading to the homes can still be seen today.

As Boyes and Agua Caliente were being developed, another promoter, George Maxwell, conceived the idea for homesites farther west of the springs and about two miles from the Plaza. The construction of a new depot for the Santa Rosa and Carquinez Railroad there made the area very desirable. Taking a cue from the number of visitors who came

TOP: Home Farm, 1917. Collection of the author.

BOTTOM: The El Verano dance hall, 1908. Collection of the author.

during the warm-weather months, he named his new town El Verano, the Spanish word for "summer." He and a number of other men formed the Sonoma Valley Improvement Company around 1887 and hired famed landscape photographer Carleton Watkins to take photos of the area's beauties to use as advertisements for both the residential lots and the resort planned for the area. In March 1888 the *Sonoma Index-Tribune* reported that a $150,000 hotel was in the works, and during the summer, land auctions were held to sell off the sites to home buyers.

El Verano eventually had its own newspaper, the *Whistle,* though it lasted only a few years. And although the town did not have the vast hot springs of Boyes and Agua Caliente, there was enough mineral water to offer visitors and residents some opportunity to take a mineral swim. It was also close enough to the larger resorts and their more expansive facilities.

El Verano had some very bad luck, however. In 1889, 1890, and 1898 fires in the area destroyed homes and outbuildings, frequently threatening the entire town. Residents kept rebuilding and the community thrived. In 1895 a camera club that toured the Bay Area on bicycles visited El Verano to take photos before biking over to the vineyards on the other side of the valley. By 1912 a family-oriented country resort called El Verano Villa opened in the area, complete with fishing, a dance pavilion, and hot mineral baths. A grammar school and a post office made El Verano a desirable place to live year-round.

Health and pleasure seekers could also spend time at Fetters Hot Springs, opened around 1907 by George and Esther Fetters in the town of Agua Caliente. They had managed a hotel in San Francisco but lost it during the earthquake and fire of 1906. They came to the area intending to start a ranch, but when they saw how popular the hot springs resorts were and discovered that the same waters were rumored to be on their land, they changed their business plan. After sinking a well and finding an abundant spring, they set up a hotel and a bathhouse with a swimming plunge. They did not give up the ranch idea, though, and managed acres of orchards, vineyards, and gardens in addition to taking in guests.

According to Dr. Sanders, another resort called Eleda Hot Springs had been on the premises before the Fetterses settled there, but it had been idle for years. The water at Fetters Hot Springs was between 108 degrees and 118 degrees in temperature, and its flow was considerable. It was faintly carbonated and the chief salts were sodium chloride, sodium carbonate, and silicon dioxide. These were best for "derangements" of the stomach and liver. According to George Fetters, his springs were composed primarily of white sulfur, which was considered beneficial for stomach and liver ailments, as well as rheumatism. He used this distinction in all of his advertising in the Sonoma and San Francisco newspapers, no doubt piggybacking on the fame of the white sulfur springs resorts in West Virginia.

It appears that Fetters, in contrast to his fellow resort owners, did not bottle and sell his water to the public. The public did come, though. The managers' club of the United Cigar Stores held its summer picnic at Fetters Hot Springs. The 350 members arrived by automobile and danced, swam, and enjoyed a picnic lunch under the oak trees. By 1917 there was a theater at the resort with dancing, motion pictures, and "the Only Original Ragtime Orchestra in the Valley."

Entertainment had become big business at the resorts, as they had started to attract visitors who sought a weekend getaway from the daily grind of business in San Francisco. Needing rest and recreation instead

Fetters Hotel, 1920s. Collection of the author.

of mineral waters for their livers, the wealthy men of San Francisco and the peninsula south of the city would send their families to one of the valley resorts for a few weeks in the summer, joining them on the weekends for a respite before returning to the office on Monday. San Francisco's famous summer fog also made it very attractive to visit the sun and warmth of Sonoma as a change of scene. The San Francisco papers regularly printed the lists of the socially prominent who visited the springs in the Sonoma Valley, as well as others around the state, in columns with titles such as "At the Resorts."

When the summer season began, newspapers also ran articles about how the locals were flocking to the resorts by the hundreds. A few typical headlines for these stories were: "Where City Folk Seek Rest," "Pleasures of Country Hold the Summer Wanderers," "Many Respond to Call of Outdoors," "Many Automobilists Make Excursions to Summer Camps and Inns."

After Jack London's novel *The Valley of the Moon* was published, its popularity and his often quoted praise of the area were also used to promote local real estate. Home lots in Oak Park, just a few minutes from Boyes Springs, were advertised in the San Francisco papers with the enticing phrase "A Summer in the Valley of the Moon Spells Contentment: Jack London."

The valley's resorts offered something that was popular with all visitors: alcohol. During the 1910s a lot of agitation took place throughout the United States about the effects of alcohol on families and society, and Sonoma was not immune. Many locals despised the alcohol-fueled revelry of the dance pavilions and concerts down the road at Boyes, Agua Caliente, Fetters, and El Verano, and vented their irritation in newspaper articles and letters to the editor.

Local business leaders knew that the resorts were a source of income, and not only at the hotels and springs themselves. Visitors also made their way into Sonoma, where they spent money in restaurants and other establishments. The *Sonoma Index-Tribune* was a solid supporter of local saloons and the more high-class bars out at the springs. An editorial in the January 20, 1912, issue, for example, quoted an article from another paper called the *Expositor*. Its writer railed against the influence of saloons, saying that the only way to combat the lawlessness that they fostered was to shut down every roadhouse in the valley. The editor of the Sonoma paper rebuked this writer in a long editorial about the city's reputation as a very law-abiding city, filled with honest, industrious, and reputable citizens.

One reason for this back-and-forth vitriol was the specter of something called the local option. In 1912 individual cities in each state could choose to enact Prohibition within their borders. The measure had to win by popular vote, and Sonoma decided on an April vote. An organization called the Men's League was in charge of campaigning for local Prohibition, and the paper took the opposite position. Nearly every issue of the *Sonoma Index-Tribune* had an article, advertisement, letter, or editorial about the subject.

When the election was held and the results announced on April 13, the paper took great glee in printing a large headline stating, "Wets Win Out Against The Drys in this City." The editor went on to write, "The election is over. Forget it. Be generous winners and good losers, to the end that peace and harmony prevail in this little community as of yore." Nationally, Prohibition took effect in 1920, and although the resorts were officially dry, plenty of drinking went on behind closed doors.

THE REMOTE LOCATION and open spaces of the springs lured another type of visitor to the area in the early twentieth century: athletes.

The first to come were professional boxers. When getting ready for big matches, many spent time at Boyes Hot Springs, living the simple life and training hard away from city distractions. In May 1908, a fighter named Eddie Hanlon spent ten days at Boyes Springs, taking long walks in the mornings and working over the punching bag in the afternoons. Two other fighters, Toby Irwin and Kid McFadden, joined him near the end of his visit and provided him with the actual fighting practice he needed. Two years later, in April 1910, English fighter Owen Moran made a flying visit to Boyes to play a game of cricket against some English visitors, returning to nearby San Rafael to finish up his daily calisthenics. Local and San Francisco papers from the 1910s are full of articles about the famous and near-famous boxers who spent time in training at the springs.

But the sportsmen who spent the most time and had the most fun at the springs were the members of the San Francisco Seals baseball team. The Seals were a minor-league team, part of the Pacific Coast League from 1903 until 1957, when they moved to Phoenix, Arizona. There was a baseball field at Boyes Hot Springs as early as 1912, and in November of that year the owners of the resort struck a deal with Seals manager Bill Reidy. Starting in the spring of 1913, the Seals would train before each season at Boyes and also play some exhibition games. Not only was there a fine baseball field for the team, but there were also plenty of rooms among all of the resorts to house the young players.

In February 1913 the Seals came to town to play against the local Sonoma Valley Stars in a benefit game to raise money for a young man badly injured by a local train. The following month the town of Sonoma nearly emptied out to watch the Seals play the Chicago White Sox at the Boyes baseball park. And although the Sox beat the Seals 4–1, a good time was had by everyone in the stands, including—according to rumor—Jack London.

The Seals made their way north to Sonoma every spring from 1913 until about 1950, and locals went to as many of their exhibition games as possible. One waitress at the camp in the early 1920s remembered that the players were on a very strict diet during the training season. Allowed only one piece of pie and a glass of milk with their lunch, for example, they often begged her to slip them an extra slice. Sympathetic with the plight of the young men, who were about her own age, she could only smile and gesture toward the team manager, who was always lurking nearby.

ENTERTAINMENT AND DIVERSIONS were especially needed during Prohibition, which lasted from 1920 until 1933. The swimming plunges, fine accommodations, and live music brought visitors and residents to the various springs over the following decades. For example, a New Year's Eve celebration in 1922 at Boyes included bonfires, community singing, card playing, concerts, and a feast, sponsored by the Boyes Springs New Improvement Club.

Resort owners were not complacent about their success, and improvement was always on their minds. Plans for a large new hotel in Boyes Springs literally went up in smoke in 1923 when a massive fire destroyed

NEW HOTEL·
AGUA CALIENTE SPRINGS

FIREPROOF
STEAM HEATED
SULPHUR BATHS
IN ROOMS · ·

TOP: The "plunge" at Fetters Hot Springs, 1920s. Collection of the author.

BOTTOM: The Agua Caliente Hotel, 1920. Collection of the author.

the existing hotel and almost the entire resort. But as soon as the debris was cleared, rebuilding began, and the new hotel, named the Sonoma Mission Inn, opened in 1927.

Tourism has to change with the times, or it quickly becomes obsolete. In the 1920s more middle-class visitors made their way to the area in cars, and auto courts like the Caliente Villa in Agua Caliente opened to serve those who had their own wheels. As a consequence, the railroad saw a bit of a drop-off in business.

By the 1940s the resorts were looking a little tired, though there was plenty of local entertainment to be had as always: movies, dances, live music, and, of course, swimming. The railroad tracks were removed in 1942, ending nearly sixty years of service. Despite the availability of motels, the tourism industry began to slow even more. The swimming plunges were still in business well into the 1970s, but the loss of the Boyes Hot Springs bathhouse to fire in 1969 and the Fetters Hotel in 1975 meant the end of an era. The former Agua Caliente Hotel became a retirement home, and is one of the few structures remaining from the old resort days.

Most of the tourists who head to the valley today aim for the Plaza and its nearby wineries and picnic areas. But the former communities of Boyes Hot Springs, Agua Caliente, Fetters Hot Springs, and El Verano still hum. Today they are filled with new residents and new businesses, many catering to the area's Hispanic population. Restaurants, movie theaters, fruit stands, consignment shops, hotels, and antiques stores supply residents' needs. And visitors who drive through on the way out of Sonoma can still stop to enjoy one final meal or drink, as the mineral springs continue to bubble beneath the ribbon of Highway 12.

Chapter Seven

More Famous Names and Faces

$\mathcal{E}$ver since the first adobe brick was set into the foundation of Mission San Francisco Solano, the town of Sonoma has been a lure for a great cross section of global society. Beyond missionaries, tourists, and entrepreneurs, Sonoma has hosted visitors and residents who hailed from the worlds of the military, business, food and wine, literature, and Hollywood. Some only passed through town; others visited frequently. A few made Sonoma their home, and one was even hauled off to jail.

Although Sonoma's first residents were men who toiled in spiritual fields, it was the military that really put the place on the map. From the day in 1833 when General Vallejo and his family arrived until the Pacific Squadron relocated across the bay to Benicia nearly twenty years later, Sonoma was a military post. After the Bear Flag Revolt, American soldiers of all stripes lived in town and left their mark on the city's history. Some of them went on to brilliant military careers in the Civil War. Among these were Philip Kearny, George Stoneman, and Charles Stone. But two achieved fame that still resonates in town today.

One was Joseph Hooker, born in Massachusetts in 1814. He graduated from West Point in 1837, and in 1849 he was named assistant adjutant general of the Pacific Division, joining General Persifer Smith in Sonoma. While in town he found a way to add to his army pay by acting as an unofficial middleman to the quartermaster. That is, he charged the military large fees for supplies like hay and firewood that he bought from local residents for a pittance. He was brought up on charges and was eventually acquitted, but he was forced to take a leave of absence from the army.

Hooker decided to stay in town despite his local reputation and managed to distinguish himself over the next few years. He served as the foreman of a coroner's jury in the case of a man accused of mule stealing who was subsequently lynched. He also ran for State Assembly, though he didn't win, and he owned a 550-acre ranch at Agua Caliente, where the Agua Caliente Springs Hotel was later built. He also built a house on First Street West in town, later selling the property and its acreage to the Vasquez family.

By the time the Civil War broke out, Hooker was back in the army, and in 1862 he was commissioned a brigadier general. He was denied promotion in 1863 and left the field service, spending the rest of the war as a departmental commander. He retired in 1868 with the rank of major general.

Before returning to the military he tried to sell his Agua Caliente property, but his land title was a little fuzzy. After the war he had to petition the Andrew Johnson administration to confirm his title, which was eventually granted. The people of Sonoma remembered him for decades, referring to him by a nickname he never liked: Fighting Joe. A wagon allegedly belonging to Hooker was used in a San Francisco parade celebrating the seventy-fifth anniversary of California's statehood in 1925. And a trunk that he left behind at his Agua Caliente property was given by a later owner of the site to the "Golden Gate Park museum" in San Francisco. Its whereabouts today are unknown.

The Vasquez House, once owned by Hooker at its First Street West site was moved to its present location in the El Paseo shopping complex on First Street East. It is now the headquarters of the Sonoma League for Historic Preservation.

One of the most famous of the Civil War generals also played an important role in Sonoma history, in an episode that veers close to farce. It involved future General "Marching Through Georgia" William Tecumseh Sherman.

After the Bear Flaggers took over Sonoma in 1846 and Commodore

Sloat had seized California for the United States, the Bears elected immigrant John Nash to act as alcalde. They felt they had the right to install an official of their own choosing because they were acting with Sloat's permission, and they believed he had authority over California. Unfortunately, that was not the case—the man who was really in charge was military governor Stephen Watts Kearny. In the spring of 1847 he appointed Lilburn Boggs to be the Sonoma alcalde and ordered Captain Brackett, in charge of the troops in town, to give Nash the news.

Nash and his Bear Flag friends were outraged. They did not feel that an American general had the right to dictate Sonoma's political activities. Kearny and Colonel Richard Mason, who would succeed him as governor, countered that California was now a province of the United States and the American military was in charge. Nash's arguments were ignored, and he was ordered to surrender his office, books, and records, and account for all money spent and received. If he didn't comply, Captain Brackett was to remove him by force.

While all this was going on, Sherman was rising in his own military career. Born in Ohio in 1820, he graduated near the top of his class at West Point in 1840. Lieutenant Sherman was ordered to Monterey, California, in 1847, and arrived there just two days before the town of Yerba Buena was renamed San Francisco. He accompanied General Kearny to Los Angeles and after returning to Monterey, he went to Sonoma to solve the Nash problem.

As he wrote in his memoirs, Sonoma was in a "dangerous state of effervescence," because Nash had so many followers in town. The transfer of power to Boggs did not look promising, though. Captain Brackett had asked to be relieved of the duty of carrying out Kearny's orders because he was a mere volunteer officer and was going to be discharged soon anyway. When Sherman heard about the situation, he volunteered to go to Sonoma to settle the matter.

He left Monterey for San Francisco to catch a boat to Sonoma, picking up another officer, Louis McLane, and four sailors to accompany him. After landing at the Embarcadero, the men headed into town on foot. They found Captain Brackett and informed him that they had come to take Nash prisoner for refusing the orders of the military governor.

Nash was unmarried and was living in a home belonging to a local lawyer named Henry Green on First Street East, just a block south of the Plaza. On the day of Sherman's arrival he was in Napa, but was expected back in the evening. While waiting, Sherman and McLane visited a local farm to buy some chickens and pigs to take back with them to San Francisco, and also spent time with Lilburn Boggs (who was no doubt on tenterhooks about actually becoming alcalde) and the always hospitable General Vallejo.

After dark, Sherman learned that Nash had returned home, and he ordered the sailors to keep a cart ready nearby on the Plaza. He and McLane went to the Green house, knocked on the door, and then walked in, finding Nash and Green having dinner with two women. Sherman asked if one of the men was John Nash, and one of the women pointed him out. Nash stood up and the heavily armed Sherman walked over and ordered the man to accompany him out of the house. "Where?" Nash asked. Sherman replied, "Monterey." When Nash asked the reason for his removal, Sherman brusquely said he would tell him later.

As they headed for the door, Green blocked their way, demanding to know why Nash was being arrested. Sherman didn't answer, simply pointing to his pistol and telling him to get out of the way. They went out the door with Green following behind and yelling, which got the attention of the sailors back at the Plaza. One of them had a pistol, which he accidentally discharged, and Green scurried back into his house.

After explaining things to Nash on the seasickness-inducing boat trip back to San Francisco, Sherman left him in the care of another officer and headed to Monterey by land. Nash arrived there via another woozy sea voyage, and when he promised to return to Sonoma and hand over the office of alcalde to Boggs, he was released. The prospect of harsh treatment by the military authorities had cooled his temper, and when his worst fears were not realized, he was ready to meekly head back home.

Sherman probably never went back to Sonoma (though he is rumored to have spent some of his time at the Blue Wing Inn), but after he resigned his commission in 1853 he returned to San Francisco and worked at the Lucas, Turner & Co. bank. He was in charge of a local militia during the activities of the Second Committee of Vigilance in 1856, and the following year he and his family left California for good. In 1861 he was reappointed to the army as colonel of the newly authorized

Thirteenth US Infantry and is remembered today as one of the Civil War's most famous officers.

The memory of yet another military man also lives on in Sonoma in the name of an important street and a popular ball field: five-star general Henry "Hap" Arnold, who created the modern United States Air Force.

A native of Pennsylvania, Arnold was born in 1886 and graduated from West Point in 1907, which is where he picked up his nickname: an abbreviation of "happy." He was assigned to the Twenty-ninth Infantry in the Philippines, and in 1911 he was detailed to the Signal Corps. For this assignment he had to learn to fly, and he was sent to Dayton, Ohio, where his teachers were none other than Orville and Wilbur Wright. By June he was proficient and he became one of the first military aviators. A stellar career followed, and by 1938 he was a major general in charge of the newly created Air Corps.

In March 1942 he became the commanding general of the Army Air Forces and during World War II he directed the air war against Germany and Japan. During his tenure the air forces grew from 22,000 officers and men with 3,900 planes to nearly 2,500,000 men and 75,000 aircraft. In June 1945 he had a heart attack brought on by overwork, and the following summer he retired from the service.

In 1943 Arnold and his wife, Bee, met Mr. and Mrs. Frank Bartholomew, who were restoring the old Buena Vista Winery. They were taken with the peace and beauty of Sonoma and purchased a forty-acre ranch in Glen Ellen that they named El Rancho Feliz. It was a nod to his nickname; *feliz* is the Spanish word for "happy." After he retired, Arnold and his wife relocated permanently to the ranch, where they daily saw deer, quail, and wild turkeys.

They loved the serenity of their life in Sonoma. Arnold spent time at the local hardware store, as well as the restaurants and bars. Other famous military men visited the couple, including Jimmy Doolittle, the aviator who was renowned for his raids over Japan during World War II; Lowell Thomas, the writer, explorer, and broadcaster; and General George Marshall, the chief military advisor to President Roosevelt, secretary of state under President Truman, and architect of the Marshall Plan, which helped Europe recover from the ravages of the war.

Arnold was also an accomplished writer. In 1928 he wrote a collection of juvenile novels called the Bill Bruce Series, which he hoped would get boys interested in the world of aviation. In 1948 Arnold published an article for *National Geographic Magazine* titled "My Life in the Valley of the Moon." It's a very personal look at bucolic ranch life, in contrast to his years in the military, which had been filled with roaring bombers and the wrangles of diplomacy. In November of the following year he published a memoir of his life titled *Global Mission,* advertised with large display ads in the *Sonoma Index-Tribune.*

By the time his memoirs appeared on bookstore shelves Arnold had been given another honor. On May 7, 1949, he was appointed the first general of the US Air Force, a five-star rank. Because he was retired, his appointment had to be authorized by a bill passed in the US Congress, which it had no trouble doing.

The years at war had taken their toll on Arnold's health, and despite the peaceful activities of his retirement years, he died in January 1950, at the age of sixty-four. President Truman sent his own airplane to Sonoma to take Arnold's body and his family to Washington for a state funeral. Hap Arnold was buried at Arlington National Cemetery, followed by his wife, Bee, in the 1970s.

Sonoma never forgot the kind and friendly military man who shared stories and the occasional beer with them over the years. Just weeks after his death a movement was launched to rename a long stretch of road in his honor. It was approved in April 1950, and today Arnold Drive stretches from the big bend near Schellville all the way into Glen Ellen. During that same month, a new athletic field being planned for Sonoma was also named for the general. Arnold Drive and Arnold Field are important local landmarks for residents and visitors alike, and many of the town's residents still remember Hap Arnold with great affection.

SONOMA'S FAMOUS food and wine culture is nothing new. From General Vallejo's legendary wine cellar to today's trendy restaurants, the city has always attracted people who personify the good life.

One of those people was the writer M. F. K. Fisher, born Mary Frances Kennedy in Michigan in 1908. Her family moved to southern California when she was a child, and it was there that she first encountered the foods and customs that would influence her future writing career. She married and in 1929 she and her new husband moved to France, where they spent three years. Her life there, learning about French wines, cheeses, and local cuisine, recalls the experiences of Julia Child, and when she and her husband returned to the United States in 1932 she began to publish essays about food and cooking.

After a painful divorce, Fisher lived throughout Europe and then returned to California, where, in 1955, she bought a house in the Napa Valley, using it as a base for further travels. In 1971 she moved to a place she called Last House, in Glen Ellen, and lived there until her death in 1992.

Her essays and books about California foods and wines sound remarkably contemporary. She championed local wines and hailed the taste and quality of Sonoma's sourdough bread and cheeses. She wrote about California cuisine in the 1970s in words still used to describe it today: freshness, availability, and simplicity.

One of the country's biggest and most well-known cookware brands got its start in Sonoma as a hardware store. Chuck Williams arrived in the Sonoma Valley in 1947 as a contractor. In 1953, after a trip to France, he opened a small shop on Broadway called simply Chuck Williams and offering "Housewares—Hardware—Paints." He placed lots of ads in the *Sonoma Index-Tribune,* in the spring advertising china, crystal, stainless, and small appliances for those who needed wedding gifts, and during the holiday season his store also offered items like candy jars and decorative bowls.

In 1956 Williams had a lucky escape when he was installing an appliance in the kitchen of his store. He was working with flammable cement and it somehow ignited, causing an explosion that smashed all of the crockery, burned the cabinets, shattered the windows, and caused the ceiling plaster to break into pieces. Miraculously, Williams was unhurt.

He moved his business to downtown San Francisco in 1958, but he never forgot where he got his start. He continued to support local youth causes and, of course, gave the Valley of the Moon the ultimate tribute when the time came to name his new company: Williams-Sonoma.

COMMERCE has always been an important part of Sonoma's history. Businesses of all types have been started in town, and merchants have been passing through Sonoma for more than 150 years. Some are obscure, and others have names that are still famous today.

Early business interests in Sonoma took many forms. Even before the first storefronts were opened on the Plaza, men saw the commercial potential of the Sonoma Valley and its environs. In January 1842, for example, Sir George Simpson, governor general of the Hudson's Bay Company, made his way to Sonoma. This Canadian firm was famous for pioneering the commercialization of the fur trade throughout North America. Now Simpson wanted permission to do fur trapping off the coast, just a short ride from the Valley of the Moon.

Vallejo had the power to grant or deny this request, so Simpson arranged to meet the general in town. After enduring an uncomfortably rainy trip across San Pablo Bay and up Sonoma Creek, Simpson and his party straggled onto the Plaza. He and the group dined with Vallejo, and Simpson was impressed with both the man and his home. He wasn't as thrilled with the spicy food he was served at dinner, though.

A San Francisco businessman whose name adorns millions of blue jeans had a few local customers in town: Levi Strauss. The Bavarian-born merchant and manufacturer advertised in the *Sonoma-Index Tribune,* and many of the stores in Sonoma carried Levi Strauss & Co.'s fine dry goods or his line of riveted denim pants and jackets.

One of them was the Poppe store, on First Street East, and Strauss cultivated a relationship with owners Julius and Catherine that went beyond business. The Poppes were from Germany, so the couple might have become friends with Strauss because of their mutual homeland. The extent of their friendship is unknown because Levi Strauss & Co. lost its historical records in the 1906 earthquake and fire. It is known, however, that Mrs. Poppe sent Strauss a case of her family's locally made wine for the holiday season in 1891. In his note of thanks Strauss said, "Although I am no wine expert, my judgment is, that California need not feel ashamed of what you are producing."

California also produced another popular product: sugar. Claus Spreckels, the founder of Spreckels Sugar Co., was born in Germany in 1828, lived in South Carolina and New York, and ended up in San Francisco in 1856 as a successful grocer. Always on the lookout for other opportunities, he opened a brewery and then began refining sugar, first with Hawaiian cane and then with California beets. By the end of the nineteenth century he was a multimillionaire with interests in railroads, steamships, real estate, banks, and public utilities.

One of his many children was Rudolph, born in 1872. He made an independent fortune in sugar and gas companies and clashed constantly with his father about business, but he was unusual in that his politics leaned toward the progressive in an era of great corruption. He was one of the men who brought down former San Francisco mayor Eugene Schmitz and his crony, machine boss Abe Ruef, after the earthquake and fire of 1906.

In 1895 Rudolph Spreckels purchased a large piece of property in Sonoma called Sobre Vista. Located in the western hills and next door to the vast property that later belonged to Jack London, the property was originally owned by General Vallejo. In 1872 the estate was acquired by George Hooper, a Virginia-born trader and banker who retired from business in 1876 and moved permanently to the area. Over the next two decades Hooper planted and cultivated a variety of cash crops on his ranch, the most successful of which was olives. He spoke frequently at meetings of local horticultural societies about the value of olives to California's economy. By 1895, however, he was spending more time in the East after marrying his second wife, and in that year he sold Sobre Vista to Rudolph Spreckels.

Spreckels had big plans for the ranch, which included raising poultry as well as continuing to cultivate Hooper's olive crops. The place also had a large and beautiful home, which Spreckels used as a sometime country place, not intending to live there year-round.

Spreckels improved the property by purchasing additional tracts of land, and when the existing house burned down in 1905, he rebuilt it on a grander scale. In 1908 three men were killed when dynamite being used to drill a well on the land exploded prematurely.

Spreckels continued to spend time at Sobre Vista into the 1920s, but after some financial reversals during the Depression he sold the house and property to his sister-in-law Alma Spreckels, the wife of his brother Adolph. Sometimes called Big Alma, she had been notorious in her youth and had posed for the statue that adorns the Dewey Monument in San Francisco's Union Square. As Adolph's wife, she used her money

and influence to benefit the city, for example through the creation of the Palace of the Legion of Honor and the San Francisco Maritime Museum.

After buying Sobre Vista from Rudolph, Alma threw her considerable energy into making even more improvements to the hillside home. The project provided work for many local men during a very hard time, and memories of Alma's generosity still linger in town. By the time she finished the renovations, Sobre Vista was a grand estate, and over the years it hosted celebrities such as Charlie Chaplin, John Barrymore, and Bing Crosby. During World War II Alma opened the house to the US Army as a recreational center for returning soldiers. Alma died in 1968, and today part of the Sobre Vista property belongs to the Sonoma Golf Club. Other portions of the land were developed decades ago for private homes.

JACK LONDON isn't the only writer who found inspiration in the Sonoma Valley. One who preceded him by half a century was Frank Marryat, an English sportsman/tourist who traveled around California in 1850–1851. In 1855 he published *Mountains and Molehills; or, Recollections of a Burnt Journal,* a vivid look at his two-year sojourn.

In August 1850 Marryat was at the Sonoma Embarcadero trying to book passage on a ship back to San Francisco after visiting nearby Napa. While waiting for the tide to turn, the boatmen had found their way to one of the houses in San Luis, which was a combination store and grog shop. Marryat went in to see about transportation and noted that the sailors were spending their time drinking Champagne and listening to fiddle music. He quickly realized that the boatmen were too drunk to manage the trip, so he decided to accompany Mr. Ramsey, the shop's proprietor—another Englishman, to a ball being held in Sonoma that evening.

They found transportation into town and booked rooms at one of the Plaza's hotels. While watching the local farmers and laborers at a public dance, Marryat made a remark in French to Ramsey, which was taken as an insult by a blacksmith standing nearby. He suggested that Marryat leave the building, which he did. Once outside, he started to look for his companion, and was then suddenly attacked by the blacksmith and three other sturdy men. Marryat wrote that the gentlemen apparently mistook his head for an anvil and began to bludgeon him before he could defend himself. (The heading for this section of his book is "I Am Left For Dead.")

The next thing he knew, he was lying in the Plaza's scrubby grass. He managed to crawl to his hotel, where he found Ramsey, who had also been looking for him. Discovering that he was stunned but not badly damaged, Marryat returned with Ramsey to San Luis. He missed the boat to San Francisco, so he had to loiter in the area for a while longer. When he finally set off in a small yawl, he noted that the three-man crew was half-drunk and didn't seem to know what they were doing. Even before leaving Sonoma Creek they managed to run the boat into the bank, where they were stuck for so long that they missed the tide and sat high and dry until it turned again.

Early published accounts of Sonoma are often anonymous. One such is a multi-part travel essay titled "A Trip Across the Bay," which appeared in the *California Star* on January 8, 1848. The writer described his visit to Sonoma and penned a couple of long paragraphs about the difficulty of getting into town from the Embarcadero: "The earth, parched and hard and the road in advance, possibly dusty; horses were not to be had, and as 'calling for cab' was more a matter of doubtful success, walk we must, and to it, after many grave suggestions, we bent ourselves, with serio-comic mein, and staggered hopes."

The writer with the most interesting name, and the most offbeat view of Sonoma, has to be George Horatio Derby, otherwise known as "Squibob." Born in Massachusetts in 1823, Derby was an army officer with a taste for practical jokes and a reputation as a wit, earned while attending West Point. He served in the Mexican War, then stayed on in California, exploring the region and sending reports back to Congress. He was then posted to California permanently between 1852 and 1856. He edited the *San Diego Herald* newspaper for a time and gave the journal a comic turn, publishing humorous essays under the pseudonyms "John Phoenix" and "Squibob."

In October 1850 he was in San Francisco and decided to pay a visit to Sonoma. The essay about his time there appeared in the October 29 issue of the *Daily Alta California,* and was also published in his collected writings, titled *Phoenixiana; or, sketches and burlesques.*

Derby's humor still shines, even 150 years after his essay was written Surprised that Sonoma was pleasant enough to tempt him to stay for ten whole days, he praised the city's climate, plant life, structures, and people. "Sonoma *is* a nice place," he wrote at the beginning of his essay.

Of General Persifer Smith's army battalion, stationed in town, he said:

"I saw a troop in the street one day. He wore a coat with a singularly brief tail, and a nose of a remarkably vivid tinge of redness. I thought that he might have just returned from the expedition, for his limbs were evidently weakened by toil and privation, and his course along the street slow in movement, and serpentine in direction."

Phoenixiana was published in 1855, and Derby died young, in 1861, leaving behind many vivid views of life in pre–Civil War California.

HOLLYWOOD has cast its eye at Sonoma over the years as well. As early as 1913 a version of Jack London's *Valley of the Moon* was partially shot at Wolf House. A decade later, in mid-November 1923, locals were thrilled to hear that members of the Redwood Film Company were in town to scout locations for a few upcoming films. The crew liked what they saw, and announced that producer, director, actor, and author Harold J. "Josh" Binney planned a visit to see the site for himself.

Binney was born in Kansas City in 1890 and got his start in the entertainment business as a vaudeville actor at the age of seventeen. By 1910 he was acting for the Biograph movie company in New York, and a few years later he started to work in California with director Mack Sennett, known today for his slapstick comedies. A large man, Binney was much in the style of the more famous Fatty Arbuckle, and he was soon producing and starring in his own comedy films. By the mid-1910s movies were labeled as "A Josh Binney Comedy," with Binney serving as producer and director, and featuring actors such as Funny Fatty Filbert.

Binney liked what he saw in Sonoma, and by December he had opened a local production office and studio at "Coney Island," a series of tent pavilions near El Verano that had been used for local entertainments. He planned to produce and film twelve silent movies in the Sonoma Valley, starting with a two-reeler called *An Account of a No Account Count*. A number of less well-known but still recognizable silent film actors invaded the valley and began to film scenes at the resorts and other local spots. A few Sonomans landed small parts in the movie, and even though Binney hurt his arm and came down with a case of blood poisoning, the filming went well and finished on time.

However, signs that something was not quite right began to surface in early January 1924. Binney spent a lot of money at Sonoma's stores and restaurants, and used a $750 check drawn on a New York bank to make payments around town. When the check bounced and Binney didn't make good on the money due, locals hushed up the incident to avoid embarrassment all around, but that was just the beginning of the bad news.

It soon came out that Binney had raised the money for his current film in Montana and then had run out on his investors. He had also promoted unsuccessful projects in Idaho, Washington, and Oregon, fleecing investors in those states as well. He was arrested in mid-January at his El Verano studio and briefly jailed in Santa Rosa until the members of his production company could raise his bail. A week later he was ordered to be extradited to Montana to face charges there, but he hired a local attorney to fight the order. When that didn't work, he fled and hid at the home of a friend in Santa Rosa. Finally discovered in early February, he was put on a train for Butte, where he was tried, found guilty of obtaining money under false pretenses, and sentenced to three to six years at Deer Lodge State Prison.

Binney's prisoner information card described him as a "Motion Picture Producer." He was six feet two inches in height, weighed 316 pounds, and had dark brown eyes and black hair. Additional information included, "Teeth good, Features stocky, Complexion Sallow." He was also still listed as an employee of Mack Sennett's production company. He began serving his sentence on May 4, 1924, and was released on parole November 3, 1925.

Production on *An Account of a No Account Count* had come to a halt when Binney's fraud was discovered, and cameramen Arthur Porchet and Ray Duhem refused to continue work until they were paid. Binney promised them their wages and they went back to the job for a while, but everything stopped when Binney was arrested. Porchet and Duhem seized the film in lieu of wages, and except for a few feet of celluloid containing some disconnected scenes, the full film hasn't been seen since.

A clever writer for the *Sonoma Index-Tribune* wrote a faux four-reel movie treatment of the Binney episode on February 9, 1924, called "Skeletonized Version of a Movie Dream." In the final "reel," the story included the following scenes:

Movie man in toils. Flees.
Spirited away by typewriter expert who had the key to situation.
Under cover.
Detectives discover him hiding at midnight.
Boards train for Montana with deputy sheriff.
Sonoma's dream fades.

After his release from prison, Binney went on to make more movies, achieving a bit of notoriety in the 1940s for films featuring African American actors, including Cab Calloway in *Hi-De-Ho* in 1947. The last trace of his Sonoma film empire burned to the ground in 1928, and Binney died in Los Angeles in 1956.

Sonoma and its environs have shown up in a few more films in the succeeding years. A brick-red house on Adobe Road between Sonoma and Petaluma was used for scenes in *The Farmer's Daughter* in 1947. *American Graffiti* featured some road scenes along Highway 121 near Schellville in 1973, and in 1982 *Shoot the Moon* used the Wolf House ruins for some of its exteriors. Sonoma's Armstrong Estates was featured in *Tucker: The Man and His Dream* in 1987, and the Sonoma Community Center showed up in *Scream* from 1996.

Locals got a big kick out of *Bottle Shock* in 2008. In this film about the California wines that beat French wines in a famous 1976 tasting, storefronts just east of the Plaza stood in for Paris exteriors, and the north side of the Plaza substituted for . . . Napa.

THE ONE CONSTANT in all of Sonoma's history, from military post to family-friendly town and popular tourist destination, was General Vallejo. For nearly sixty years, he gave his time, his money, and his reputation to the city, and in doing so, he helped set the course of California's history.

The Bear Flag Revolt of 1846 helped usher in the American takeover of California, assisted by the victories in the Mexican War and the increased population of the Gold Rush years. Vallejo was very pleased when he was invited to be a delegate to the first constitutional convention in 1849, and even more delighted when California became the thirty-first state in September 1850.

He should not have been surprised. The part he played in keeping the revolt from becoming a bloodbath, and the dignity he showed during his incarceration, were well known to the Americans who flocked to California and Sonoma in the late 1840s. As early as 1847 he was profiled in Robert Semple's *Californian* newspaper, having obviously impressed the newspaperman during his association with the Bears.

Unfortunately Vallejo did not truly prosper once California joined the Union. His reputation was secure, but his finances were not. And although his generosity was appreciated, it was not always returned.

While attending the first constitutional convention, Vallejo served on committees for finance, elections, and preparing documents in Spanish. And on November 13, 1849, he was elected a state senator. The following year he offered the state 156 acres of land near the Carquinez Strait for a new capital, which he wanted to call Eureka, but his fellow politicians suggested he name it after himself. He also offered thousands of dollars to the legislature for the construction of buildings suitable for the new seat of government.

But there was no consensus among the legislators about where the new capital should be. Beginning in 1850, California's political center bounced around the north from San José to Vallejo to Benicia (named for Vallejo's wife, on land that once belonged to the general) to Sacramento, settling there permanently in 1854 (with a short stint in San Francisco in 1862 during a bad flood year).

Vallejo lost both money and prestige during this process, and he decided that one term as state senator was enough. He was also disillusioned by the loss of some of his land titles and the financial failure of his ranch in Petaluma, which he was forced to sell in 1857.

After leaving the legislature, he began to devote more time and energy to his new home and estate at Lachryma Montis, as well as the town of Sonoma itself. In 1852 Vallejo was elected the city's mayor, and he began the next phase of his life as beloved elder statesman and city benefactor.

This role was nothing new. In 1847 Vallejo had heard about the plight of the Donner Party, trapped in the Sierras by a fierce and unexpected autumn snowstorm. When a second relief expedition was being organized, he contributed money—some say as much as $5,000—to help outfit the rescuers. In November, two of the four orphaned daughters of George and Tamsen Donner, Eliza and Georgia, were adopted by a Sonoma couple, Mr. and Mrs. Christian Brunner, who operated a local dairy. Eliza Donner wrote an account of her time in Sonoma, remembering her adoptive parents with affection.

Even after retiring from politics and devoting himself to life in Sonoma, Vallejo was not forgotten. Visitors to Sonoma always seemed to end up on his doorstep. In 1848 an anonymous writer for the *California Star* came to town and visited "the affluent and hospitable Gen. V." He and his companions were received "with that peculiarly bland sincerity with which his numerous guests are courteously welcomed, and agreeably entertained." Vallejo's status as one of the founders of California was secured when he was elected a vice president of the Society of California Pioneers in 1850.

By the 1860s Vallejo had added horticulturist to his list of accomplishments. His winemaking had achieved some fame at county and state fairs. And in 1861 an article about Lachryma Montis appeared in the *California Farmer and Journal of Useful Sciences*. The writer was astonished at the extent of Vallejo's agricultural estate, which included 10,000 grapevines, pear, plum, cherry, and peach trees, and vaults containing ten 500-gallon barrels of wine. In 1865 Vallejo reported that he had gathered 2,100 pounds of apples from one eighty-year-old tree located on the Lachryma Montis property. His home and its surrounding orchards and vineyards were not only practical but also beautiful, as illustrated by the writer's comment that "the peach trees looked like pyramids of pink floss."

But influence did not mean wealth. After statehood, and as he watched his former landholdings diminish in the American court system, Vallejo and his wife made ends meet by selling produce to local hotels and selling water from the spring above his home to the town of Sonoma. The worst came to pass in 1866: Vallejo lost his ownership of Lachryma Montis and was forced to pay rent to the new mortgage owner. But in 1871 Vallejo's son-in-law John Frisbie managed to purchase the property and then deeded it to the general's wife.

Vallejo may have been bitter about how America repaid his efforts to help the country acquire California, but he rarely expressed it openly. He saved most of his opinions for his memoirs and other historical writings that he both published and shared with writers over the years. And then he just got on with his life, though occasionally he dipped into the past.

In 1874 he wrote a letter to the *Sacramento Daily Union* newspaper regarding recent articles printed about a California Indian known as Marcelo, who had fought with Vallejo against Estanislao in 1829. Baptized at Mission Santa Clara in 1789, Marcelo spent his life allied with Spain and Mexico during their Indian wars. In his letter Vallejo said, "Please go and see him in my name, and if possible induce him to accept during a week, a month, or a year the hospitality which I cheerfully offer him in my retreat of 'Lachryma Montis.'" Marcelo died the following year.

By the early 1880s Vallejo was enjoying himself as a member of the California State Horticultural Association, and was frequently sought out for his opinion on important matters. In 1888 he suggested that the state be divided into sections and at least six pest inspectors be hired to watch for dangerous insects (the *Phylloxera* infestation no doubt was uppermost in his mind). He also attended a number of events put on by the Native Sons of the Golden West and the Society of California Pioneers.

In August 1888 three hundred members of the National Educational

Association visited Sonoma, and a group of female teachers called on General Vallejo. He showed them around his orchards and vineyards, and as they were getting ready to leave, one young woman impulsively kissed the eighty-one-year-old general on the cheek. The entire delegation immediately followed her example, and the pleased Vallejo endured a shower of kisses over the next few minutes.

In January 1890 Vallejo was reported to have been ill and confined to bed for a couple of months. However, by January 15 newspapers printed stories that he was in much better health, with an improved appetite. But three days later he died in bed at his beloved Lachryma Montis.

His death was reported in papers not only in California cities such as San Francisco, Sacramento, and Los Angeles but also in Honolulu, Wichita, Salt Lake City, and New York. He was eulogized for his contributions to the development of California and for his status as a descendant of one of the first families of the old province. He was a "wellbeloved warrior, statesman, native son and citizen."

The general was buried in Sonoma's Mountain Cemetery on January 21, 1890, and his funeral was attended by locals and prominent people from around California.

General Vallejo at Lachryma Montis, 1887. Courtesy Sonoma Valley Historical Society. Used by permission.

The life of General Vallejo was celebrated during a California Admission Day parade in September 1908. His grandsons Carlos and Raoul led the four white horses pulling Vallejo's own carriage, which was decorated with his portrait. Collection of Joseph T. Silva. Used by permission.

Many people would speak or write about Vallejo in the following years. An American named Charles Wilson, who started a dancing school in 1840s San Francisco to teach American dances to Mexican families, wrote in March 1900 that his favorite pupil was General Vallejo, and that all the ladies liked dancing with him because he was courteous and handsome. The famous opera singer Adelina Patti, who sang in San Francisco in 1884, once told a story about dining with Vallejo that was printed in *The Century Illustrated* magazine in 1891. She asked him if he had enjoyed the first opera he ever heard. When Vallejo replied that he hadn't, she demanded to know the details of when and where. He told her that it had taken place in 1828 at the site of the future Palace Hotel in San Francisco. When she asked him for the name of the prima donna he said he couldn't remember, but that "there were at least five hundred coyotes in the chorus."

Today, all fourth-grade students in California study the state's history, and General Vallejo's life and activities are always part of the curriculum. His relationships with the Indian population of California, at his Petaluma rancho and through his secularization work at the Sonoma mission, are a greater part of the story than they were in the past. To some, this tarnishes his image, but in truth he was simply a man of his time and of his culture, and all new information helps make him more real to today's visitors. His life, and his choices, made Sonoma what it is today.

The restoration of the Sonoma mission during the early-twentieth-century revival of interest in California's Spanish past. Courtesy Sonoma Valley Historical Society. Used by permission.

Epilogue

THE VALLEY OF THE MOON

$\mathcal{S}$onoma is home to a fascinating mixture of multigenerational families and brand-new residents. Small as it is—the population hovers around 14,000—Sonoma offers everything that modern living requires, and augments that with the visible remnants and intangible benefits of its long history.

During the 1960s, Mission San Francisco Solano, the former Mexican barracks, the Toscano Hotel, the Blue Wing Inn, the two-story servants' quarters from the old Casa Grande (called Casa de Criados), and Vallejo's Lachryma Montis all became part of the Sonoma State Historic Park. Archaeological work at the various sites over the past forty years has given historians new insight into the city's past.

In 1999, for example, more than 150 years of Native American anonymity was rectified when members of the Coast Miwok, Patwin, Wappo, and Pomo tribes placed an elegant monument outside the west facade of the mission. Carved into granite are the names of nearly one thousand Indians who were buried on the property without markers and without memory. Exhaustive research into mission records revealed hundreds of names of the dead, which now live forever in stone.

Only first names are used—those given to the converts by the padres—and they are listed chronologically by the year of their death. For example, between 1824 and 1839 the dead included the child Franca

Solana, the adults Capistrano and Olimpia, and another child named Exutino. Though long overdue, the monument is a poignant reminder of the city's First Peoples.

Many of the structures that ring the Plaza, and those that surround it throughout the valley, serve a very different purpose than their builders originally intended—the sign of a healthy and thriving city. The former train depot, moved away from the Plaza in 1890, now houses the Sonoma Valley Historical Society, in the appropriately named Depot Park. The former Carnegie library is now the Sonoma Valley Visitors Bureau, and restaurants now live where general stores used to be.

The wine industry, dating back more than 150 years, is part of Sonoma's lure, and it continues to grow. This long and sophisticated involvement in food and wine culture led to the city's early adoption of the concept of using local foods and sustainable agriculture, known as "slow food." The commitment to sustainability brought Sonoma a great honor in 2009: Cittaslow International, the organization that advocates for the slow food movement, named Sonoma the first Cittaslow city in the United States.

Jack London's books still thrill readers today, and the California State Park established in 1960 at what is now called his "Beauty Ranch" sees

The former railroad station is now the Sonoma Valley Historical Society's Depot Museum. Courtesy Sonoma Valley Historical Society. Used by permission.

thousands of visitors every year. The cottage where he died, filled with the artifacts of the *Snark* voyage, the stone Pig Palace, and Charmian's House of Happy Walls illuminate the lives of the couple who could have lived anywhere.

London once wrote that Sonoma was a "golden land," and nearly two centuries after its founding, it has not lost its shine. Here in the Valley of the Moon, soldiers, writers, farmers, moviemakers, entrepreneurs, and urbanites alike have realized, and continue to realize, their California dream.

Bibliography

Primary Sources

NEWSPAPERS

The Californian
Daily Alta California
Pacific Rural Press
San Francisco Call
Sonoma Index-Tribune

GOVERNMENT DOCUMENTS

Directory of the Grape Growers and Wine Makers of California. Sacramento: Board of State Viticultural Commissioners, 1888.

MANUSCRIPT MATERIAL

Beebe, Rose Marie, and Robert M. Senkewicz, eds. *Testimonios: Early California Through the Eyes of Women, 1815–1848.* Berkeley: Heyday Books, 2006.
Osio, Antonio María. *The History of Alta California: A Memoir of Mexican California.* Translated, edited, and annotated by Rose Marie Beebe and Robert M. Senkewicz. Madison: University of Wisconsin Press, 1996.

Secondary Sources

Adler, Jacob. *Claus Spreckels: The Sugar King in Hawaii.* Honolulu: University of Hawaii Press, 1966.
Alexander, James B. *Sonoma Valley Legacy: Histories and Sites of 70 Historic Adobes in and Around the Sonoma Valley.* Sonoma: Sonoma Valley Historical Society, 1986.
Alley, Lynn. "Researchers Uncover Identity of Historic California Grape." *WineSpectator.com,* February 12, 2007.

Arnold, H. H. "My Life in the Valley of the Moon." *National Geographic Magazine,* December 1948.

Brady, Roy. "The Swallow That Came from Capistrano." *New West,* September 24, 1979.

Bryant, Edwin. *What I Saw in California.* Lincoln: University of Nebraska Press, 1985.

Coffey, Thomas M. *Hap: The Story of the U.S. Air Force and the Man Who Built It, General Henry H. "Hap" Arnold.* New York: Viking, 1982.

Deutschman, Alan. *A Tale of Two Valleys: Wine, Wealth, and the Battle for the Good Life in Napa and Sonoma.* New York: Broadway Books, 2003.

Eargle, Dolan H., Jr. *Native California Guide: Weaving the Past and Present.* San Francisco: Trees Company Press, 2000.

Early, James. *Presidio, Mission, and Pueblo: Spanish Architecture and Urbanism in the United States.* Dallas, TX: Southern Methodist University Press, 2004.

Haley, James L. *Wolf: The Lives of Jack London.* New York: Basic Books, 2010.

Hart, James D. *A Companion to California.* Berkeley: University of California Press, 1987.

Haslam, Gerald, ed. *Jack London's Golden State.* Berkeley: Heyday Books, 1999.

Haughey, Homer L., and Connie Kale Johnson. *Jack London Ranch Album.* Stockton, CA: Heritage Publishing, 1985.

Hayes, Gregory W., and Matt Atkinson. *Jack London's Wolf House.* Glen Ellen, CA: Valley of the Moon Natural History Association, 2010.

Iverson, Eve. "Wine at the California Missions." California Mission Studies Association, 1998.

Jacknis, Ira, ed. *Food in California Indian Culture.* Berkeley: Phoebe Hearst Museum of Anthropology, University of California, 2004.

Kropp, Phoebe S. *California Vieja: Culture and Memory in a Modern American Place.* Berkeley: University of California Press, 2006.

London, Jack. *The Valley of the Moon.* New York: Grosset and Dunlap, 1913.

Lynch, Robert M. *The Sonoma Valley Story: Pages Through the Ages.* Sonoma: Sonoma Index-Tribune, 1997.

McGinty, Brian. *Strong Wine: The Life and Legend of Agoston Haraszthy.* Stanford, CA: Stanford University Press, 1998.

O'Hara, Joy. "The Jack London Guest Ranch." *Hoofs and Horns,* October 1935.

Overland Monthly. Jack London Edition, May 1917.

Parmelee, Robert D. *Pioneer Sonoma.* Sonoma: Sonoma Valley Historical Society, 1972.

Peninou, Ernest P., ed. *History of the Sonoma Viticultural District: The Grape Growers, the Wine Makers, and the Vineyards.* Santa Rosa: Nomis Press, 1998.

Pinney, Thomas. *A History of Wine in America: From Prohibition to the Present.* Berkeley: University of California Press, 2005.

———. *A History of Wine in America: From the Beginnings to Prohibition.* Berkeley: University of California Press, 1989.

Reardon, Joan, ed. *A Stew or a Story: An Assortment of Short Works by M. F. K. Fisher.* Emeryville, CA: Shoemaker and Hoard, 2006.

Reesman, Jeanne Campbell, Sara S. Hodson, and Philip Adam. *Jack London, Photographer.* Athens: University of Georgia Press, 2010.

Rosenus, Alan. *General Vallejo and the Advent of the Americans.* Berkeley: Heyday Books, 1999.

Scharlach, Bernice. *Big Alma: San Francisco's Alma Spreckels.* San Francisco: Scottwall Associates, 1990.

Schoenman, Theodore, ed. *Father of California Wine, Agoston Haraszthy, Including Grape Culture, Wines, and Winemaking.* Santa Barbara, CA: Capra Press, 1979.

Smilie, Robert S. *The Sonoma Mission: San Francisco Solano de Sonoma.* Fresno, CA: Valley Publishers, 1975.

Stasz, Clarice. *American Dreamers: Charmian and Jack London.* New York: St. Martin's Press, 1988.

———. *Jack London's Women.* Amherst: University of Massachusetts Press, 2001.

Street, Richard Steven. *Beasts of the Field: A Narrative History of California Farmworkers, 1769–1913.* Stanford, CA: Stanford University Press, 2004.

———. *Photographing Farmworkers in California.* Stanford, CA: Stanford University Press, 2004.

Webb, Edith. "Agriculture in the Days of the Early Padres." *The Americas* 4 (January 1948).

———. *Indian Life at the Old Missions.* Los Angeles: W. F. Lewis, 1952.

Index